The Shared-Meal Revolution

How to Reclaim Balance and Connection in a Fragmented World through Sharing Meals with Family and Friends

Carol Archambeault

Illustrations by Edgar Mayorga

authorHOUSE®

AuthorHouse™ LLC
1663 Liberty Drive
Bloomington, IN 47403
www.authorhouse.com
Phone: 1-800-839-8640

Published by AuthorHouse   10/24/2013

ISBN: 978-1-4918-2294-4 (sc)
ISBN: 978-1-4918-2293-7 (e)

Library of Congress Control Number: 2013917757

This book is printed on acid-free paper.

The Shared-Meal Revolution

For my parents, Elizabeth and Phillip, for all the meals they shared with our family, extended family, friends, and neighbors over the years. The thousands of conversations we had during our family's shared meals will always hold a special place in my heart.

For everyone who believes that achieving balance and connection through shared meals is a worthy pursuit.

Contents

Acknowledgments

A sincere thank-you to those who have supported and helped with this book project in a variety of ways: Linda Peace, Dora Garza, Angela Congelose, Bonnie and Tim Scoville, Chef Elyse Lain Elshenawey, Tim Flynn, Rob Ripley, Edgar Mayorga, Jeff Richards, Che Newton, Jennifer Pullinger, Olga Mansuryan, Martha Clark, Deb Brewer, Josh Hamilton, Diana Luc, Jerry and Pat Scoville, Barbara Biziou, Sergio Lopez, Pacific Oaks College, and the many relatives and friends who have honored me over the years with their presence at shared meals. Special thanks to Jane Cruz for her gracious, insightful, and thoughtful feedback. Love and thanks to my brothers and sisters: Bill, Peachy, Phil, Myra, Vera, Jim, Frankie, Mary, Joey, and Carl who offered a great deal of honesty and candor about their experiences at our family table. A special shout-out to my twin, Carl, for helping me with technical issues and for always being the best brother a girl could have. My heartfelt gratitude to Elizabeth Richards ("GSTQ!") without whose help I could not have finished this book. Her guidance, support, expert eye, humor, and worldly perspective helped tremendously to clarify ideas and concepts.

Thank you to the two dearest people in my life: my daughter, Jini, and my son, John. I'm deeply grateful for the love we have for each other and for the meals we share. You are beautiful, courageous, and truly awesome individuals. I thank my lucky stars that I have the privilege to be your mom.

Introduction

When I walk into my kitchen today, I am not alone. Whether we know it or not, none of us is. We bring fathers and mothers and kitchen tables, and every meal we have ever eaten. Food is never just food. It's also a way of getting at something else: who we are, who we have been, and who we want to be.
—Molly Wizenberg

Around the Dinner Table: My Story

It has been said that a person is born twice: first at birth, and again when her mother dies. This was certainly true for me.

During my mother's last years of life, her brain was ravaged by Alzheimer's disease. As the disease progressed, she could enjoy fewer and fewer activities. Her communication skills diminished, and making any kind of connection with her seemed increasingly futile to me, my ten siblings, and our father. However, she enjoyed one activity until the end of her life: *sharing meals.* Family members who lived nearby developed a rotating schedule so that one of them was with her during mealtimes. They shared food, conversation, and laughter with her, and at the end of the evening meal, they helped her settle in for sleep.

Considering her inability to communicate during these last meals, it would be impossible to prove that my mother consciously connected with us, but during those precious last days of her life, we felt a deep sense of connection and peace. At last, we were reciprocating the gift of the shared meal—a gift she had lovingly dedicated to each of us for more than thirty years.

My brother Jim, who is sixth in the birth order of my siblings, was sharing a meal with our mother one day before she lost her ability to speak. The two of them were alone in the room. Between bites, and to Jim's great surprise, our mother said sweetly, "I love you."

Jim said, "I love you too, Mom."

She quickly replied, "What makes you think I was talking to you?" and they both began to laugh hysterically.

This is one of the last times anyone recalls my mother speaking more than a single word at a time, and soon she stopped speaking altogether. It is significant to me that this exchange took place during a shared meal, because laughter at the family dinner table is something I remember vividly from my childhood. It reminded my siblings and me of similar exchanges when we were children. We looked forward to mealtimes for feelings of love and engagement and the pleasure of our mother's occasionally wacky sense of humor.

During my mother's last days and in the days following her death, I felt a strange lack of connectedness with my friends and family members. I was at a crucial time in my life when I was examining my choices, my future, and my identity, and I felt unsure about the direction my life should take. As I struggled to end the malaise and uncertainty of my continuing life vision, I had the urge to reconnect with others by sharing meals. Several years, many delicious meal gatherings, and about eighteen pounds later, I realized I'd been actively seeking to relive the shared mealtimes of my childhood. By sharing meals and discussing life events with others, I rekindled childhood feelings of pleasure, comfort, and security. I soon realized I'd been using shared meals to explore my options as I faced a life transition. I had unconsciously resurrected the shared-meal activity as a way to regain momentum and move forward.

Since this time of rediscovering shared meals, I have developed a passion for helping others become aware of the benefits. I have also refined my meal planning to make better choices about nutrition, health, and weight management.

I attended college in my forties and studied human development, a field concerned with observing and analyzing human behavior and the influences and changes that people experience throughout a life span. When it was time to choose a topic for my master's thesis, I decided on the ritual of family meals.

Now a fifty-one-year-old single woman living in Southern California, I have raised two children—a daughter, Jini, who is twenty-eight years old, and a son, John, twenty-five, both of whom have lived in California for the majority of their lives.

I was raised in the once heavily industrialized New England city of Bristol, Connecticut. Our household consisted of my parents, my six brothers, my four sisters, and me. My twin brother and I were the two youngest children in the family. Frequent visitors in our home were our maternal grandparents (Italian immigrants) and our paternal grandparents who came to the United States from Canada and had some Native American lineage.

Our parents, blue-collar, working-class people, had themselves been brought up during the Great Depression of the 1930s. They realized parenting a family of this size would definitely be challenging in many ways. As you might imagine, simply maintaining order in a house overflowing with activity was a masterful endeavor requiring strategy, planning, and creativity throughout the many years children were in their care (from the late forties to the early eighties).

A family meal ritual was one tool my parents used to keep track of their large brood. Throughout my childhood, I experienced firsthand the importance of gathering at the table. My mother and father thoughtfully planned our mealtimes and regularly communicated about our various assignments. The older children helped by planning menus, shopping, and preparing food with our mother. The younger children learned table setting skills, transferring serving bowls, and clearing the dishes.

It was understood we would all be present at the dinner table at five o'clock. Extracurricular school and personal activities were scheduled around mealtimes.

There were a few financially challenging years for my parents in which they had to work different shifts at their respective factories. During these years when my mother was working second-shift hours, my father stepped up with loving enthusiasm to lead the dinnertime brigade.

On Sunday afternoons, we often held a larger dinner party that began at two o'clock and often lasted through the afternoon. These meals usually featured a guest of honor—a relative, a neighbor, someone from our church, or a sibling's new "love."

On some weekends, we traveled to relatives' homes. Gatherings at an aunt's or uncle's house provided various people (twenty or more) passing through the kitchen all day. We prepared familiar Italian specialties, such as *pizza frite*, *pasta e fagiole*, or *pizzelle* treats. The men swung by to roll some dough, boil some pasta, or comment expertly, "*Abundanza!*" Everyone gathered at an oversized table for a bite to eat, taking a break from bocce ball, horseshoes, or a game of tag. With so much family, it seemed it was always someone's birthday or there was an occasion of some kind to celebrate. Those times were filled with fun, laughter, friendly gossip, and delicious food.

I remember many important conversations that took place around the family dinner table. We discussed with anticipation the upcoming weddings of my older siblings. One evening, one of my brothers announced that he would be entering military service. On another memorable occasion, my mother broke a painful silence about the death of her only sister. My mother was a selfless woman, not one to draw attention to her needs, but at supper that night she spoke tenderly about how it felt to lose someone she held so dear and told us how she was healing. The fact that she chose dinnertime to discuss her feelings made her comments seem especially significant to me.

But dinner at our house was rarely so solemn. Far more often it was a celebratory, lively, and rambunctious time. My mother was proud of her Italian heritage, and I grew up understanding that the good-natured teasing and jovial spirit at our table were typical characteristics of the Italian culture. The room always felt full, and the magnitude of the event seemed larger than life.

Once dinner was served, a steady stream of bowls and platters would be passed around the table for everyone to serve himself. After this occurred, our parents would scan the crowded table, being sure everyone had food on his plate. The meal experience would be off and running for the next hour or so. At the table, there were laughs, colorful stories, and the prevailing sense that we were each other's keepers. If any of us needed a sounding board, there were plenty of volunteers. Because we were such a large family and getting all of us together in one place every day could present its challenges, dinnertime was an effective way to stay in touch. During the dinner hour, there was no rushing off to a friend's house to watch TV or any familiar dings of today's electronics. If someone called on the house phone or knocked at the door, one of my parents would leave the table and address the caller and let them know we were busy having dinner; the call would be returned as soon as dinnertime was over.

Of course, we were not a flawless group. The frustrations of a challenging life occasionally erupted in our otherwise loving father's demeanor at dinnertime. For the oldest group, and in the earliest years of our family's ritual, there were rules and regulations that often made the mealtime environment feel tense for them. The five oldest of my siblings recalled a different experience at the table than the youngest six siblings and I. But the lasting impression from all eleven children was the deep admiration of my parents for their commitment to our meal ritual and to the well-being of our family. This ritual made us feel part of something special. Before each other's eyes, all thirteen of us were developing as individuals and growing together as a unit.

My four sisters and I experienced special times with our mother in the kitchen where we learned family recipes that we would later pass down to our own children. At every Friday evening meal, Mom performed her apple-peeling art; we marveled as she peeled the fruit with a tiny knife while making only a single tear in the skin. My seat at the dinner table was always to the right side of my mother, and I still picture her sturdy hands placing the dome-like apple peel she had created in the center of the table for all to admire.

We can all look back on our childhoods and recall the details relevant to our families. Perhaps they're very similar to what my family experienced, or perhaps they're very different. That's the beautiful thing about developing a meal ritual—every family has its own identity. Therefore, the ways you experience your ritual are dependent upon the people involved and what elements make the ritual meaningful to you.

Given my childhood experiences, the family meal ritual naturally remained an important tradition when I became an adult. After I married in the early 1980s, sharing meals was a routine practice for my growing family. It was simply expected—both culturally and personally—as a natural extension of my husband's and my backgrounds. When our children were small, we routinely shared meals without even the thought of a structured plan.

Our lifestyles were uncomplicated then. The time-management problems we had then seem quaint when compared to today's norm. We hadn't yet become entranced by the wired lifestyles many people are attached to today. Further, it seemed the ante on working so much and so hard all the time wasn't embedded in our culture.

Unfortunately, I was divorced in the early nineties, largely due to us marrying very young and not having some of the same values in mind. Determined to mitigate the disruption that divorce brings, my efforts to maintain ritualistic activities (including sharing meals with my children) became heightened in importance. My children and I shared breakfasts and weekday evening meals without fail during their early and middle childhood years. I learned over a plate of linguine that my son was becoming less interested in baseball and more interested in music and liked to find interesting ways to spike his hair with gel. I learned that my daughter had natural singing abilities and liked to express herself by wearing lots of jewelry, and her friends were experimenting with makeup. Over dinner, my children regularly challenged me to spell new words on their vocabulary lists so that we could announce to the world—or at least the small section of the world present at our table—that I was still "Speller Mom." And, it was at our dining room table that I learned the pop culture expressions my children and their friends were using so I could stay attuned to their language. I practiced their lingo, which provided my kids with hours of listening entertainment.

In addition to these lighter moments, having meals with my kids gave insights into their unfolding lives. I got a read on their relevant developmental issues and had the opportunity to show my support. At times I learned details that triggered an intervention or prompted me to suggest solutions. For example, during middle school, my daughter, Jini, was being pursued by a boy who had a wild crush on her. He was following her home after school. This was causing some anxiety for her and all the parents too. Another time I discovered my son, John, was enjoying a stint as class clown, and I gathered from his colorful stories that his antics were lighting up the classroom now and again. I realized I should give his teacher a call. I used family mealtime as an opportunity to monitor and support their growth during these important years. The bonus was that it did not strain my budget or my time—a prime concern for me, because as a single parent I had limited amounts of both.

Even though my kids and I made concerted efforts to keep up this tradition—as did their father in his own single-parent household—as time passed and they reached their high school years, we found it more and more difficult to make sharing meals a priority. Increasingly, conflicts pulled us away from the family table. At times, there was a work assignment that kept me late at the office or some other professional or academic endeavor I was pursuing to improve our family's quality of life. Other times, my son's basketball practice, my daughter's choir rehearsal, and a myriad of other commitments scheduled in the early evening hours would leave us with an empty seat at the dinner table. We had become hyperscheduled. We were starting to feel our shared meals being squeezed out from our lives.

Eating was becoming just another activity, and we would find ourselves increasingly grabbing food on the run.

Although our schedules sometimes conflicted during the week, we would still have three or four meals together, even if it meant we were waiting for John to finish a school-site council meeting or for Jini to come home from dance practice. We tried to be flexible, especially during the weekdays when it was harder to get together. We were more successful in slowing the pace on weekends, allowing us to share a leisurely Saturday evening supper or a Sunday breakfast together. Whenever I began to feel particularly distanced from my children, I would find a way for us to share an emergency meal. I remember one such time when my son and I met my daughter at a show choir dress rehearsal so we could share sub sandwiches and enjoy catch-up conversation during her break. But this was only a temporary fix and did not satisfy the longing to be around the dining table together.

There was still no specific plan to ensure we were making time to share a meal once a day, and I (in my own overscheduled frenzy) never considered designing one. We were simply coping and hoping for the best. Without a plan, our lifestyles would continue to eat away at our intention to gather daily for a meal. Not surprisingly, the same challenges were affecting the lives of every family I knew.

What This Book Is About

Once upon a time in America, sharing meals with others was the norm. Families routinely ate together, inviting relatives, friends, and neighbors to break bread with them. Allowing someone to eat alone was viewed as downright uncivilized.

Today, practicing a shared-meal routine is subject to fierce competition from many influences that challenge our good intentions:

- We are overscheduled and exhausted, be it from too much work or too many activities.
- Mealtime has become another chore on our to-do list.

- We are depreciating our meal experiences with fast, cheap food in order to save time.
- We are often too busy to stop and think about what really matters; our values lack definition and focus.
- We are overdependent on technology to help us stay connected.
- We're lacking the type of intimate connection people get when they are face-to-face.

As a casualty of our hyperactive lives, we are neglecting a proven relationship-building activity: sharing meals. We want to feel connection with those we love and have the satisfaction that we are taking care of ourselves and our families. Workable for all, regardless of family structure or domestic situation, sharing meals is a positive strategy to revive wholeness in what is a sadly fragmented American lifestyle.

A revolutionary plan for sharing meals addresses what we can do to become a more intact American society, engaged in the daily welfare of our loved ones. I strongly believe we can again find the treasure of life balance by sharing meals with our families, spouses, friends, and members of our community, allowing us to reclaim something essential to our long-term well-being—interpersonal connection. Sharing meals is a powerful step we can all take to cultivate a stronger and more positive American culture.

Benefits of shared meals explored in this book include nurturing social skills, developing the art of communication, building positive self-esteem and identity, feeling stable and secure, living in the moment, finding sanctuary in spiritual unity, exploring our creativity, understanding the link between food and nature, and bonding with ancestral history and traditions.

I'm inviting you to join *The Shared-Meal Revolution*. Embrace the spirit you'll find in this guided journey of important insights, examples, and exercises. Enriching your life through the daily practice of shared meals is my promise—a more fulfilled life is your reward.

Carol Archambeault

A Brief Look at the History of Sharing Meals

The practice of eating together began as a survival strategy among prehistoric peoples. It continued well after the shift from hunting and gathering to a focus on improving agricultural methods. For countless generations, communities collaborated by farming the land to meet common needs. Sharing food was only one manifestation of the connection between families, the larger community, and nature.

Later, in the nineteenth century, the Industrial Revolution drastically began to change the way people ate and the company they kept while eating. Industrialization spurred a movement away from rural, small-scale, farm-based livelihoods to urban, modernized ways of working and living for those employed in places like offices or factories. Everyday attitudes toward domestic household life started to change too.

Changes in the workforce offered these new urban workers more purchasing power. Products were quickly being manufactured and marketed to them for consumption. Factory and office workers looking for an efficient workday lunch took advantage of convenient solutions such as self-service cafeterias, "automats" (vending machines), luncheonettes, and diners, which developed a growing presence in cities beginning in the 1880s. Adding to the landscape of dining convenience was the fast-food craze, the kernels of which began in 1923 with the opening of an A&W Root Beer drive-in in Sacramento, California. However, it wasn't until the early 1950s that franchises such as McDonald's gained a significant place in American culture.

Food delivery services (such as pizza and Chinese food) became more common in the late fifties and into the seventies, as did dining establishments featuring take-out meals. These new alternatives were efficient, convenient, and cheap—prices were low due to the mass production of the food products used. These food choices appealed increasingly to middle-class households who had more disposable income and to women workers (slowly increasing in numbers) who also juggled domestic duties. Over the years, methods of eating became more complex, resulting in a depersonalization of the meal experience.

Our current eating practices reflect these characteristics, only amplified by the passing of decades. The way we eat today can be summed up by saying we eat a wide variety of industrialized food in a vast manner of individualized ways.

Many people choose to leave home for the workday without eating anything. They grab a coffee and muffin from one of the popular coffee chains and swoop into work for a quick "deskfast." Others eat something from the drive-through on their way to work or school. When my children were young, my ex-husband often dropped the two of them off at our child-care provider's home before school, donuts in hand. She'd tease him by pointing out they were getting their "daily dose of vitamin D."

During a typical workday, many adults eat midday "meals" in their offices or at their workstations, basking in the glow of their computer screens, dining "al desko." Some workers can't spare the time to stop for lunch, so they snack mindlessly throughout the day.

For people of all ages, sit-down meals are becoming scarcer in favor of our expanding appetite for snack foods. An unfortunate by-product of frequent snacking is it can easily diminish an appetite for dinner.

For those who are hungry by dinnertime, take-out food is a popular dinner choice. For some families, parents will dutifully collect an assortment of burgers or tacos from fast-food joints en route to an after-school activity. Others buy prepackaged TV dinners for family members to microwave when the mood strikes them at some point in their evening. Still others manage to prepare something delicious in their own kitchens, but instead of gathering, family members eat in shifts before racing off to their own rooms or activities.

People live under the same roof, but they are not eating with one another and may not be interacting in the home at all either.

In some households, members eat separately in order to save time to complete their personal obligations. Parents modify their behaviors in an effort to "make everyone happy." My sister told me about a coworker who has adopted a food court approach in her home. She places a large platter offering a wide variety of foods—ranging from fried chicken to Chinese take-out to pizza slices—in the center of the dining table next to a stack of plates and a box of utensils. She sends a text message to everyone that says "Food!" and waits for her four kids to whisk down the hall to the table. She stands by in hope of a thirty-second conversation. Other than this impromptu check-in, "just to see if they're still alive," she has little or no interaction with her children for the rest of the night.

This mother, like many others, is trying her best to develop workable strategies. But trends like these are disconcerting. How did the American dinner hour turn into a scenario like this? How did the way we make and eat food become so passionless? I recall a commercial for Wendy's hamburgers in which an elderly woman staring into an open hamburger bun demands, "Where's the beef?" I see our empty dining tables across America and wonder, "Where's the soul?" How we are choosing to eat is speaking volumes about the value of our social ties.

I think most people understand, consciously or unconsciously, that sharing food is an important activity to our overall well-being. As journalist and food activist Paul Roberts said, "For eating is the most basic interaction we have with the outside world, and the most intimate." Clearly the choices we make about *how* and *what* we eat carry both personal and cultural meaning.

In their book *Food, Society, and Environment*, Charles Harper and Bryan Le Beau write, "Eating with others transforms biological hunger into indicators of social relationships." The choices we make when sharing food reflects how we feel about the relationship. Many of us (unconsciously or with intent) choose the manner in which we share food or drink based on the meaning we want to convey. For example, my daughter recently visited home with her boyfriend during a break from a music contract. She wanted to introduce him to our family traditions by serving some "legacy dishes" in our home. In contrast to that meal, my brother asked me to greet his business partner who was in town for a couple of days. Not having met this man before, I decided to join him at a restaurant that I knew was friendly and casual, rather than hosting a dinner at my house. These two examples illustrate how the ways in which we share food carry social meaning.

Sharing food with others has been made complicated today by the glut of food choices in the marketplace. Roberts argues the meaning associated with food has been turned inside out. He notes that "food cultures that once treated cooking and eating as central elements in maintaining social structure and tradition are slowly being usurped by a global food culture, where cost and convenience are dominant, the social meal is obsolete, and the art of cooking is fetishized in coffee-table cookbooks and on television shows."

Home cooking has been pushed aside by an astounding amount of market alternatives. These alternatives include low-cost, highly processed items by food manufacturing giants. Some of these products come out of the microwave with "grill marks" and offer the crispiness of food associated with real cooking. The genius marketing of these food products is that they give those eating on the run a simulated experience of a homemade meal.

It's easy to see how we have become confused about our food ways, because food choice and meal experiences can feel blighted in today's marketing-hyped world. Our current approach to eating leads to what Leon Kass, PhD, a culture critic at the University of Chicago, calls "spiritual anorexia." Kass says we "still eat when hungry, but no longer know what it means."

What is at stake if we grow accustomed to eating in this transient way, consuming most of our meals alone with only the sound of the microwave timer to keep us company? What happens to us, individually and collectively, when we allow the ritual of sharing meals to fall away? If we treat meals casually, we are diminishing the value of the many elements of a meal's experience—food preparation, cooking, and dining. In effect, we're cheapening the very way we live and relate to one another.

In this book I illustrate that when we abandon this ritual, we deny ourselves an obvious opportunity for care, companionship, and connection, which are as necessary to our survival as the actual food we eat. Fortunately, we can begin to again forge intimate bonds through eating together if we choose to.

The fact that you are reading this book shows a tremendous investment in yourself, your family, and your friends. It also shows you care about the society you live in and want something more than the status quo. Stopping to truly think about what brings you joy in your everyday life also shows a commitment to living out your potential, and I applaud you for taking this first step.

There's a new mood in the air. Many of us are examining our schedules and rethinking how we want to spend our precious time. A movement is happily afoot that encourages us to slow down and reevaluate our priorities—in other words, to balance our lives. I offer that life balance includes strategies to share meals with others.

When we gather to nurture each other through food ways, we are creating wealth and long-term equity in our relationships. And in a world that appreciates sound investments, who can argue with a return like that?

Thoughts from My Children

Though I was confident the meals my children and I shared helped form a solid foundation of support for their lives, when writing this book, I asked them how they felt our meals specifically affected them.

My daughter, Jini, immediately said she learned empathy, recalling the times we talked about something that happened at school. She said our talks at the table taught her to consider her teachers' viewpoints. John, my son, primarily felt our meals helped him develop an appreciation for good quality food and the ceremony of gathering together. Jini added she felt we were an intact family despite having grown up in two single-parent homes. She said she learned to be accountable for her behaviors, both at and away from the table. They felt our family meals helped them learn to express themselves and to be open about others' ideas. They also said they learned how to be a good friend and to be there for each other.

They enjoyed experimenting with ingredients and taking part in menu planning and had some fond memories of doing this. Today, Jini shows creativity in cooking and looks for opportunities to prepare and share food with others. John leans toward helping with the atmosphere of the meal, although he's learned to make a few things in the kitchen and is growing more comfortable cooking each year.

Both Jini and John easily expressed affection for the times we spent together around the table. They've grown to be loving, communicative, emotionally stable, goal-oriented, creative, and kind. They pay attention to their well-being and act with caring intent for people in their lives. Sounds something like a parental wish list, but truly, besides being dear to me because of our blood relation, I find them to be two of my favorite people.

I attribute the good nature of their company (at least in part) to the thousands of times we spent laughing and sharing around the dinner table during the formative years of their childhood. Another distinction is that they are two of the best active listeners I have ever encountered. Further evidence of the impact of our shared-meal ritual is that whenever any important event is occurring in their lives, they instinctively turn to sharing a meal to make a connection.

I consider myself fortunate that my children received the benefits of shared meals. It is my goal to bring awareness to others about the power of this wonderful ritual. I have received the benefits throughout many stages of my life: first in my childhood, then when raising my own children, and currently in my adult life as a single woman. It is my passion to share my experiences.

Share. Connect. Simplify.

I am starting a shared-meal revolution beginning with a national dialogue about this important topic. The three words that are at the foundation are: share, connect, and simplify. That is, *share* a meal with someone else, *connect* with others over a shared meal thereby receiving support from and giving support to the people you care about, and *simplify* your life by focusing on only those activities that provide life meaning and purpose for you.

Sharing meals is a relevant practice that benefits personal and family well-being and creates a healthier society. Let's make this "old-fashioned" ritual a modern, preferred lifestyle *choice*.

Recently, I became an Italian citizen and therefore enjoy dual citizenship in Italy and the United States. I admire the Italian culture, and even though some might consider it singularly focused on pleasure, there's much more to it. Italians celebrate the beauty found in everyday living, as well as nurturing relationships with others. I'm not saying that Americans don't care about relationship building; I believe we do. But it doesn't seem personal relationships are the *top* priority.

If we encourage it, the return to the once-natural custom of sharing meals as a prominent activity can permeate our culture with more energy than the launch of the latest tech tool or a record-breaking day on Wall Street. Let's practice sharing meals with the same investment we show in our careers and with the same dedication we practice being dutiful consumers.

Planning, preparing, and eating meals with others can be as simple or as extravagant as you wish. You can design your shared-meal practice to fit your unique preferences. You can develop a shared-meal plan by cherry-picking the options that work best for you.

For families, I believe it is critical to the welfare of growing children to share at least one meal a day, whether that is breakfast, a midday meal, or dinner. If you're part of a couple, be sure you are regularly strengthening your relationship through a shared meal with your significant other. If you're a single person, find opportunities to experience interpersonal connection over meals with roommates, relatives, friends, neighbors, and colleagues as often as possible to engage with and support one another.

Let's give this ritual the prominence it deserves. This is positively an achievable goal, which I am happy to have outlined for you throughout this book.

Here's how we start.

Let me take you through the steps of rediscovering, planning, and implementing a shared-meal practice. You'll find easy-to-use exercises and relevant resources you can explore to help you understand how sharing meals will greatly enhance your life.

Welcome to the table!

Exercise: Soup's On

You'll need a journal, notebook, or computer to write your answers to the questions below. If you use a computer, start a file and add to it as you complete the exercises in each chapter. (Note: This exercise is available on my website at http://www.shared-meals.com/tools.)

Take a few minutes right now to think about your own experiences with food growing up. What were some of your favorite things to eat? What were some of your least favorite things to eat? Did you share food with anyone? Did anyone cook for you? Did you cook for anyone else? Did your family share meals or have other rituals that revolved around food? Do you have generally positive or negative memories of eating with other people? Write down whatever comes to mind, whether it is a list of words or phrases, a drawing, or a story.

Step 1

Understanding the Significance of Shared Meals

The destiny of nations depends on the manner in which they are fed.
—Jean Anthelme Brillat-Savarin

Like most Americans of the baby boomer generation, I began sharing meals in childhood in the context of family life. When planning the research for my master's thesis, my own family provided the perfect subjects to interview, given that we had practiced a strong family meal ritual, there were so many of us, and we spanned several generations. We also enjoyed a wide range of perspectives and personal experiences shaped by the time periods in which we had grown up.

Although my study focused on the family meal ritual, the results and my supporting research also allowed insights into the value of sharing meals for couples, single people, and older members of our communities. I learned that through this simple shared-meal ritual, we can enjoy a unique, highly connected experience with a wide variety of benefits. Another result of my research was the development of strategies for sharing meals. I also identified some common pitfalls that sometimes affect people's ability or willingness to share meals.

In my study, I asked the following question: "What is the single most important aspect of family meals?" My family members gave various answers:

- being together as a family
- interacting with parents
- bringing everyone together
- being heard and listening
- revealing how everyone's life is going
- stopping everything else to be together
- enhancing feelings of security and family identity
- being together as one family but unique as individuals
- knowing what is expected and knowing our limits
- learning to express oneself
- understanding how family members represent themselves to the world as a family
- communication and communion

There were some notable differences between the oldest siblings (who grew up in the forties and fifties) and the younger ones (who grew up in the sixties through the early eighties). In the earliest years, the oldest group of siblings felt the meals together were stressful, largely due to rigid cultural norms of the day, although that improved as the years went by. The younger siblings group (of which I am a member) had a positive experience from the start. The lasting impression of all ten of my siblings is that shared meals are a valuable ritual linked to shared group identity, feelings of belonging, and a loving commitment by parents to their kids. They each practice a shared-meal plan with their own families, preserving many aspects of the family meal ritual we enjoyed. The group also agreed the ritual has lost its prominence in American culture because of our frenzied pace, overcommitted schedules, and the widespread view that individual freedoms are privileged over communal interests. I found the youngest generation of my family members (the children and grandchildren of my siblings) expressed concern about a shared-meal plan inhibiting their personal freedom, but they simultaneously worried about losing connection with family members.

My siblings had various ways of describing current cultural attitudes about sharing meals, from society being like a kid with attention deficit disorder to being so busy that we forget the simple everyday things, such as spending time with our family members. One brother felt having a shared-meal ritual encourages a focus on the family unit versus becoming overly self-involved. He expressed that sharing meals is valuable in teaching children that they are members of a group and not alone in the world.

Another brother felt that some problems keeping people from eating together are the increase in the divorce rate and more women in the workforce. He also suggested parents today have less "talent" than our parents in terms of exercising authority. As a result of this lack of leadership, he said kids today are missing out on opportunities to be with their families, including at the dinner table.

Another of my brothers felt that leadership in family meals is akin to talking to your kids about drugs—even if they act uninterested, it's good for them.

Sharing meals is about recognizing one another's humanity and communicating our evolving life stories. In the movie *Shall We Dance*, the character of Beverly Clark, played by Susan Sarandon, says, "We need a witness to our lives." Witnessing through a shared family meal is one way a family's overall life story is shared from one generation to the next. The dining table acts as host for family members to talk about important matters and personal interests, to develop listening and language expression skills, and to observe cultural and societal norms. In addition, parents can help guide the direction of their kids' life goals.

Studies undertaken by respected researchers and universities, including Columbia, Harvard, and the University of Minnesota, show that regular family meals are linked to healthy nutrition, strong social skills and cohesiveness, positive emotional and mental health, positive academic performance in adolescents, stronger family relationships, happier marriages, deeper connection to ethnic and cultural identity, enhanced feelings of spirituality, and reduced risky behaviors and substance abuse in teens.

Shared meals are certainly about much more than the physical act of eating food in the same room together. In today's world we acknowledge and celebrate families composed of a diverse demographic of people who may be related (or not), who may live together, or who are just friends and neighbors. But they are a family by virtue of their commitment to love and care for one another. Shared meals are for *every* family.

If the habit of sharing meals produces such wide-ranging benefits, what happens when that civilizing influence disappears? Being a civilized society is important, especially for those raising the next generation of adults who will be responsible for making future decisions that will impact us all. A child whose family doesn't fulfill essential needs for personal identity, safety, security, and belonging may develop a fragmented sense of self. He may become unable to interact well outside the walls of his home.

The absence of shared meals in a child's life can result in detachment from the family, or other unintended consequences. Adolescents, in particular, are more likely than younger children to create an alternative family reality—sometimes in a street gang or clique. The children at risk for negative behavior fall all along the socioeconomic continuum (from underserved, low-income families to affluent ones).

Infrequency of shared meals can impact the relationship of teens with their parents. According to a study from The National Center on Addiction and Substance Abuse at Columbia University (CASA), teens who have fewer than three family dinners per week describe their relationship with their parents as "fair or poor." Compared with those who have five to seven shared dinners with their parents per week, these teens are more likely to say they have "excellent" relationships with their mother and father.

In addition, teens who have fewer than three family dinners per week say they are more likely to have access to drugs—which is obviously counterproductive in building a civil society.

Further evidence to support sharing meals with children is offered by Steven J. Wolin, a clinical professor of psychiatry at George Washington University Medical Center, who says, "The family meal teaches children about behavior in a social group, and those who don't grow up with this have problems interacting in society." According to Lionel Tiger, a professor of anthropology at Rutgers University, children who eat with their families only on special occasions (such as holidays) often feel that "daily domestic life doesn't matter and that the adult world doesn't include them."

More and more, overextended parents are looking for alternative ways to take care of dinner duty. As a result, some children are managing their own needs by preparing meals for themselves and their younger siblings.

Capitalizing on this trend, many food companies have developed highly processed heat-and-eat meals that come in bright, playful packages designed especially to entice children. This strategy appeals to the child and to the parent who gets the relief of "handling" dinner duty. Marketing that targets our youth is big business. In a Federal Trade Commission report, forty-four companies spent more than 1.6 billion advertising dollars targeting children and adolescents.

Ultimately, these types of food products suggest that it's preferable for children to be responsible for their own meals, even at a very young age. This misrepresents what current psychological research tells us about the support children need from their families if they are to develop in a healthy manner.

The Dangers of Social Isolation

Americans are so driven to manage the activities packed into their schedules that they are often not meeting their own basic needs, such as sufficient rest and social connection. When faced with one more obligation, a person may ask reflexively, "What's in it for me?" Fortunately, when it comes to sharing meals, there is something in it for all of us: satiating physical hunger, experiencing many developmental benefits, achieving meaningful interpersonal connection, and living a balanced life.

In spite of the many social networking tools at our fingertips these days, Americans have never been less interpersonally connected. Harvard psychiatrists Jacqueline Olds and Richard Schwartz point out that the number of one-person households in America increased every decade between 1940 and 2000, rising from 7.7 percent to 25.8 percent. According to 2011 census data, 28 percent of all households in the United States now consist of those who live by themselves; they often reside in big cities, and the majority are middle-aged women.

According to sociologist James Cote, this social shift represents a widespread trend that he refers to as "social atomization"—people occupying private physical spaces and concentrating more on their own individual lives.

Gone are the days of block parties to celebrate a neighbor's high school graduation or the birth of a granddaughter. Communities may still gather in sincerity following a local tragedy, but to routinely meet to pursue common goals or interests is becoming a rarity. Similarly, although people might meet up with another to see the latest flick, fewer come together for more sensitive social reasons, such as visiting a sick neighbor or supporting a friend or relative during a personal crisis. You might say we are becoming accustomed to keeping to ourselves. Robert Putnam, a political scientist and the author of the book *Bowling Alone*, notes that in the past twenty-five years, "The number of people who say they never spend a social evening with a neighbor has doubled," and the time that Americans spend having an everyday conversation with another person has decreased by 25 percent.

Good social relationships, Putnam says, are strongly associated with health. In general, he says, "If you belong to no groups but decide to join one, you cut your risk of dying over the next year *in half*." Olds and Schwartz cite similarly dramatic findings: "Positive social relationships are second only to genetics in predicting health and longevity in humans," as reported from a workshop on attachment and bonding. Putnam warns, "Erosion of social capital has measurable ill effects." Research shows the power of social connectedness is something we ought to seriously consider.

In a study of the psychological effects of isolation, social psychologists Roy Baumeister and Jean Twenge found that "social exclusion" (essentially being "left out," whether self-imposed or caused by rejection by an outside community) can create a variety of self-defeating behaviors, including aggression, poor cognitive performance, and a mind-set that "avoids meaningful thought, emotion, and self-awareness." According to their study, the overall effect of social exclusion is that it seems to create a tendency in people to "give up and stop trying." Baumeister and Twenge found that these behavioral effects appeared independent of any depressed state or low level of self-esteem resulting from the exclusion itself. They found that social exclusion "dramatically changes how people function without their noticing that they feel particularly badly about it."

Olds and Schwartz chalk up the high level of social isolation in American culture to the "perpetual tension between freedom and connection." They say: "People in our society drift away from social connections because of both a push and a pull. The push is the frenetic, overscheduled, hypernetworked intensity of modern life. The pull is the American pantheon of self-reliant heroes who stand apart from the crowd. As a culture, we all romanticize standing apart, and long to have destiny in our own hands. But as individuals, each of us hates feeling left out."

There are many positive attributes about American society. But the bottom line is socialization is crucial to our country's health so that we don't deny ourselves a supportive, integrated culture.

Technology now plays a growing role to help us feel part of the world around us. Tools such as texting, Twitter, YouTube, Pinterest, Facebook, and LinkedIn purport to fulfill our need for connection with others. While their formats boast ease and efficiency, they are shallow substitutes for face-to-face time with another human being. When people turn to sites like Facebook or Twitter to satisfy an urge to connect with many friends at the same time, they are responding to the cultural "push" Olds and Schwartz describe—that is, to pack as much activity into a day as humanly possible. Social media's features—such as the ability to post a personality profile, photos, and catchy quotes—also appeal to the cultural "pull" of standing apart from the crowd and displaying one's individuality.

People are indeed fulfilling social needs through electronic means, but those needs may not be the ones they are longing to fulfill. No matter how many times we feel the temporary rush when clicking our mouse to "like" someone (or follow, retweet, mention, or pin) in a virtual transaction, we're only scratching the surface at the heart of the matter: *connection*. Researcher Brené Brown, who studies human connection, says, "Connection is why we're here . . . . It's what gives us purpose to our lives." So why are we relying on less intimate ways to stay connected?

When used to excess, virtual networking seems to reflect a symptom of a lonely society desperately seeking contact with someone. Techno-psychologist Patricia Wallace, who runs the Johns Hopkins Center for Talented Youth, compares the compulsive nature of sending electronic messages to playing a slot machine: "You are not sure you are going to get a reward every time, or how often you will, so you keep pulling that handle."

Virtual networking tools do not satisfy the human need for intricate communication and intimate connection. Many people today rely on social media as a means to meet *all* their social needs. But true socialization has a strong emotional component, and virtual messaging lacks intimacy and, therefore, real emotion. Given the impersonal nature of communicating virtually, how satisfying can this really be?

In a PBS documentary about the terrorist attack on September 11, 2001, Rabbi Irwin Kula spoke of the impact of this event on his worldview. He felt the tragedy starkly illustrated not only the fragility of life but also the deep connection among people. His insights into the frantic 911 calls of those trapped in the World Trade Center towers revealed more than desperation, fear, and declarations of love; they reflected a plea for human connection in their last moments of life. Even those who couldn't reach loved ones fulfilled connection through strangers, emergency dispatch operators, or whomever they could reach.

Despite personal differences, we are all in this life together. During ordinary times, maintaining a feeling of unity can be difficult. Do we spend much time pondering our mutual responsibility as one American people? It seems we think about what we have to do each day, we separate in our daily activities toward those pursuits, and we end up proceeding in a quasi-robotic manner, often in some form of activity cut off from others. Then, intense tragedies, such as Hurricane Katrina, the Sandy Hook Elementary School killings, or the Boston Marathon bombings, seismically jolt us from our routines and remind us of our profound link to one another.

There is a universal desire for all of us to be truly *seen* by others. It's a very fundamental aspect of our being and the difference between "Hey, how you doing?" and "I see you—and value who you are." The importance of this acknowledgment is heightened for children who are developing their identities. Think about the message a child receives when a parent lovingly honors a commitment to his well-being, including through the habits of a daily shared meal. In contrast, imagine a child's perception of himself (and ultimately his worldview) when the parent is absent and doesn't make time to be part of his daily life. The way the world greets a child conditions him to carry that same energy into adulthood. Are we greeting the youth of tomorrow with smiles or indifference?

It's time we realize our lives are intertwined, and not just in the ways we virtually wire to one another. Despite how much fuel there is to blaze a personal path of achievement, we need to find ways to connect with each other daily. Through a shared-meal practice, we embrace an attitude of inclusion. We also create solidarity, an important feature of a close-knit society. Our presence during shared meals illustrates what really matters to us.

The Happiness Equation

Many of us don't know how to meet our own needs, perhaps in part because we haven't defined what our needs really are. We all seek happiness—that elusive state of mind. But what are we doing in our daily lives to help us feel pleasure or joy? Many of us work extended hours because we believe there's a sure path to personal fulfillment through money. We believe that if only we had enough money, we could satisfy all our worldly desires. True, people may feel excitement when their income increases—money provides more economic freedom—but having more and more money, by itself, does not correlate with more and more happiness.

A worldwide Gallup poll examined the connection of happiness with higher income and enjoyment of life. It was found while "life satisfaction" increases with higher income, important daily "positive feelings" of contentment with life are strongly influenced by one's control over his life and being respected and supported by others. David Brooks, an op-ed columnist for the *New York Times*, noted, "Once the basic necessities have been achieved, future income is lightly connected to well-being." According to Brooks, research paints a portrait of contemporary culture as "oriented around the things that are easy to count, not around the things that matter most." One study on happiness found that "joining a group that meets even just once a month produces the same happiness gain as doubling your income." It turns out that "sex, socializing after work and having dinner with others" lead to the highest levels of happiness. This research strongly supports that meaningful social connection has the strongest influence on whether we feel fulfilled.

As I've seen the decades pass in my life, I've examined the times I've felt the most content and joyful. My income has modestly increased over the years, and I'm pleased that I am able to travel on special vacations and to occasionally enjoy live entertainment, such as a concert or play. I'm certainly more fortunate than many that I've been able to afford these treats. I also realize I could have been pursuing promotions and increasing my income considerably if I'd always focused on climbing the career ladder. But I've never felt it was the best trade-off—a lot more time and attention away from my home versus a better quality of relationships with those in my life. I don't want my gravestone to read, "She spent fourteen-hour days in the office and turned in thousands of high-quality reports." The memories that I have of times I felt happiest always involve my experiences with family and friends, often in everyday situations. A musician friend described his life as being "juicy" when it was full of activities that allowed him to spend time with others. I'd like my gravestone to read, "She lived a juicy life."

We can improve our happiness relatively easily by focusing on what makes us inwardly rich: our connections with people we love. Dan Buettner, a modern-day American explorer, has identified Blue Zones, which are areas of the world where the population is characterized by longevity and a high quality of life. In addition to making many positive nutrition and lifestyle choices, Buettner recommends spending at least a half hour a day with your "inner circle," as well as engaging in ritual activity: "Make one family meal a day sacred."

Considering the significant benefits that result from sharing meals, it's time to reclaim this practice and bring it back into the mainstream.

Exercise: Food for Thought

Take some time to assess how you feel after reading this chapter. Check the boxes that apply to you and complete any corresponding statements. Write your responses in the notebook or computer file you used for the introduction exercise.

List A: Questions for All
- ☐ This chapter helped me to realize that sharing meals with others has far-reaching effects. What struck me especially was:
- ☐ I want my family meals now to be like the family meals of my childhood in the following ways:
- ☐ I want my family meals now to differ from the family meals of my childhood in the following ways:
- ☐ I have family stories or stories about my past that I've never told anyone I currently know. I'd especially like to tell the stories about:
- ☐ I feel the tension between my desire for independence and my need to be connected to others. Right now, my need for _____ seems to be winning.
- ☐ There are times I long for the company of a member of my family or a good friend. Within the next few days or weeks, I'd like to get in touch with:
- ☐ I realize that I have been equating money with happiness, but no matter how hard I work or how much money I have:
- ☐ When I read that joining a group increases happiness, I thought of joining:
- ☐ The trend toward social isolation has affected me in the following ways:
- ☐ I'd like to spend less time using social networking technology and more time:
- ☐ Reading this chapter made me want to set up a schedule to share meals, and I specifically thought of:

List B: Additional Questions for Parents
- ☐ As a parent, I think of shared meals as the perfect time to teach my children about:
- ☐ My child seems to be at risk for going outside the family to meet the need for belonging. My reasons for thinking this are:

Exercise: Come and Get It

Using a chart like the one shown in Appendix A, record the frequency of your current shared-meal practice during a two-week period. (Note: You can download a copy of this Frequency Survey online at http://www.shared-meals.com/tools.) Check the box next to the type of meal you share with one or more people (breakfast, lunch, dinner).

In the space provided below the chart, describe any specific conflicts that kept you from sharing a meal with someone (for example, "worked late through dinner," "commuting," "schedule conflict," "too tired," or "unprepared").

Step 2

Recognizing the Developmental Benefits of Shared Meals

The world begins at a kitchen table.
—Joy Harjo

When I did my study on family meals, the results confirmed what I had read in literature: shared meals have the potential to benefit development in multiple ways at all stages of life. Sharing meals is relevant to literally everyone—child, adult, parent, single person, or elder. Its importance is not limited to families with children, although the intersection of shared meals and human development is particularly important to parents, because they help shape their children's habits during the crucial early years of life. The sooner people are introduced to the practice and benefits of sharing meals, the sooner it becomes a precious, lifelong habit.

What Is Human Development?

Human development is a field that combines sociology, psychology, anthropology, and biology. People who study human development are interested in how biological, cultural, and environmental influences shape individuals and communities.

According to general theories of human development, we pass through largely predictable stages from birth until death. Our lives are marked by interwoven periods of growth and stasis. Parental influence during childhood is considered a major factor that shapes lifelong choices and habits. Many adults seek continued ways to be inspired, grow, and develop throughout the middle years of their life. Elders also have unique and specific phases of development. In their later years, when they engage in daily activities that add personal meaning, they experience more enjoyment and are better prepared to accept the end of their lives peacefully.

Part A

Social Development

What we do to our children they will do to society.
—Pliny the Elder

There is strong evidence that sharing meals helps to develop children's social skills. Children who participate in shared meals acquire and practice table etiquette, learn to express themselves at the table in socially appropriate ways, and participate in what sociologist James H.S. Bossard called a "personality clinic." Food greases the wheels of conversation, encouraging people to socialize without a purpose other than experiencing one another. Sidney Mintz, professor of anthropology at Johns Hopkins University, says, "Interaction over food is the single most important feature of socializing."

During the earliest years of my family's meal ritual (the forties through the late fifties), my parents focused solely on directing the table conversation, guiding us to speak succinctly, teaching us good manners, and encouraging us to understand current events. When the six younger siblings (including me) joined the family table during the late fifties through the early eighties, our parents' (and society's) guidelines for proper behavior had relaxed considerably. At this point, we enjoyed a broader range of the social benefits of shared meals.

My siblings recalled that the family meal had significant impact on our social development. For example, my brother Ned said that interacting with a wide variety of personalities at our dinner table helped him to be comfortable in many social situations. My brother Tim added that it was a definite aid for speaking in large or public meetings and gave him nuanced social skills he uses in his sales career.

One of the most important social skills we learn by interacting with others face-to-face is the dynamic of give-and-take. Showing interest in others, knowing how to take turns—in other words, learning to share—is something we're supposed to be taught as young children. Throughout life, sharing is an important aspect of learning to live with others. Russell Belk of the University of London in Toronto suggests that sharing can result in "an expanded sense of self that embraces other people more than other things." He adds that examples of threats to sharing caused by changes in our society include "individualization of family meals."

Sharing of ourselves interpersonally isn't as high a priority these days. Just look around at personal laptops, bedrooms with personal television sets, personal cell phones, personal boxed meals, personal *everything*.

Social networking is a hugely popular and contemporary example of sharing. It is appealing and very useful, but it has its limitations and doesn't truly replace meaningful socialization.

Communication: A Two-Way Street

Communication is the foundation of social development, although even delivering what seems like the simplest message can be challenging. Whether communicating in person or through the many alternative forms now available, misinterpretation can occur. Distance communication is relatively abstract, because so many clues to meaning are left out. Most of us have had the unfortunate experience of misinterpreting an e-mail or a text message. The problem is the receiver of an electronic message must supply from imagination the missing clues the information channel does not carry, and this process can distort the meaning. Would the same message have been clearer if the sender and receiver had been in the same room? Communicating clearly to one another is vital, because each of us has a deep need to be understood.

Most facets of interpersonal experience have no dependable substitutes in written or electronic form. Telephone conversations depend solely on speaking and hearing, without seeing facial expressions and body language. Facebook and other social media transactions rely on the visual interpretation of images and written words. The video feature of Skype gets us two senses closer to being together by allowing people to see images and hear voices. But when sharing meals, all of the senses are engaged.

The senses are good at reading body language—picking up subtle changes in posture, gesture, facial expression, and vocal modulation and other physical cues, including grooming and even clothing choices. According to Olds and Schwartz, an area of the brain called the orbitofrontal cortex processes this information in order to fully socialize an experience. In less scientific terms, we get the whole picture. We benefit from a more nuanced experience.

Sharing meals can be a deeply personal experience. As the renowned food writer M. F. K. Fisher said, "Sharing food with another human being is an intimate act that should not be indulged in lightly." In her childhood, American-born Fisher ate a regimented and bland diet prepared by an older relative. Through more liberated food experiences as she grew older, she came to recognize the connection between food and emotional closeness to others.

Many infants begin forging intimate bonds through breastfeeding, and in adulthood, we still feel the pleasure of being satisfied and cared for in intimate ways. Author Naomichi Ishige, who writes about Japanese dietary patterns and symbolism, theorizes that "sex and food are the two principal bonds that hold the family together."

Of course, food is the only one of those two bonds shared among all family members. We each belong to several social groups; one such group may consist of those who eat together, which Ishige refers to as the "*kyoshoku shudan*" or "conviviality group." He also points out that "conviviality" is a trait particular to the human race and that the family system should be protected through family meals. Ishige says the shared meal is a primal activity that provides a unique format for communication within a group. In effect, food becomes a way of transmitting emotions, creating cohesion, and strengthening deep connections. Likewise, *The End of Food* author, Paul Roberts, calls eating "the one cheap pleasure that could ever rival sex." When sharing a meal, we're sharing sensations, memories, and associations.

After a shared meal with someone, we often feel relaxed, centered, and comfortable, and there's a good chance we'll end the meal feeling renewed. While there may not be inspiring conversation every time, meals together offer regular opportunities to practice the complex skill of communication. In my study of family meals, my brother Tim put it this way: "We need to sit and talk about things. Family meals are a perfect time to have conversations. There's community and caring about one another. What is accepted at the family meal table will typically be what is accepted socially out in the world."

It is because we want to have standards in our society that we provide guidance in our homes. If we treat those inside our homes in an impertinent way, we will likely treat others outside our homes that way too.

Americans have been trained to find quicker ways of doing things wherever possible. We may not readily see the benefit of spending time to communicate leisurely with others, even those we love. To the time-strapped individual, even a modestly lengthy dialogue can seem like a labored process. When my children were teenagers, there was a time when they used the word "go" in conversation to speed our exchanges along. They expected the no-frills version of whatever information I was delivering and became quite impatient with a "too-long" explanation. Understandably—they had things to do! I told them the cue "go" was uncomfortable for me, as it made me feel pressured and somewhat disrespected. They agreed to be more patient. Their impulse drove home the extent to which communication norms were changing in late twentieth-century American culture.

The main purpose of dialogue between parents, children, significant others, friends, and colleagues isn't to deliver a steady stream of information as an Internet browser does. By defaulting to a "search results" mode of communication, we miss significant opportunities to relate to each other. The purpose of dialogue is to ensure understanding, which leads to quality relationships. Sharing meals provides a wonderful venue.

In addition to personal relationships, communication skills honed during shared meals can benefit professional relationships. Quality communication is indispensable in the workplace.

As someone who has worked for broadcast media companies for the past twenty years, I'm aware of how important clear communication is to everything we do. During my career, I've observed that what comes first—before the business plans, strategizing, sharing of data, and number crunching—is simple conversation. As in the home or between friends, maintaining effective communication is necessary to create structure in a dynamic environment. Successful businesses rely on employees to communicate expertly as they implement strategies to meet goals and gain profit.

A strategy employed in some workplaces is for coworkers, project teams, and entire departments to share group meals. Some departments will host a premeeting breakfast to encourage networking immediately before a business meeting starts. While this provides an opportunity to increase commitment to company goals, it also deepens relationships and opens new channels of communication.

Sharing lunch with coworkers or potential clients has occurred for decades; it's long been called the "power lunch." Still an efficient way to satisfy hunger, conduct business, and nurture relationships, meals with coworkers can also provide a welcome break if work is not the only topic of conversation. Many workplaces have a common room for sharing food—although, regrettably, often with a television as the centerpiece of the room. Resisting the urge to turn on the tube can help you bond with a colleague over lunch.

The more we practice communicating in person, the better we become at developing what Edward Thorndike, a prominent psychologist at Columbia University during the 1920s, termed "social intelligence." The contemporary psychologist Daniel Goleman, author of *Emotional Intelligence* (1996) and *Social Intelligence* (2006), describes social intelligence in the following way:

> The ingredients of social intelligence as I see it can be organized into two broad categories: social awareness, what we sense about others—and social facility, what we then do with that awareness.
>
> Social awareness refers to a spectrum that runs from primal empathy (instantaneously sensing another's inner state), to empathic accuracy (understanding feelings and thoughts), to social cognition ("getting" complicated social situations).
>
> But simply sensing how another feels, or knowing what they think or intend, does not guarantee fruitful interactions. Social facility builds on social awareness to allow smooth, effective interactions. The spectrum of social facility includes self-presentation, influence, concern, and synchrony (interacting smoothly at the nonverbal level).

Thorndike stresses the usefulness of these skills in a range of professional positions, especially leadership roles. His analysis may be even more relevant today than in the twenties, considering the competitive nature of the job market.

Sharing meals is the perfect method to develop intuitive and rational skills that lead to social intelligence. When sharing meals, we cannot help but strengthen interpersonal bonds at home, in our neighborhoods, or at work.

Exercise: Spilling the Beans

(Note: This exercise is available online at http://www.shared-meals. com/tools.)

Exercise A: For Parents

Which social skills listed below do your children display during meals?
- ☐ following directions
- ☐ understanding the kind of physical behavior that is appropriate at the table (for example, eating with silverware, chewing with the mouth closed)
- ☐ listening attentively
- ☐ listening without interrupting
- ☐ making periodic eye contact when listening or talking
- ☐ talking so that others can understand
- ☐ answering questions when asked
- ☐ taking turns in conversation
- ☐ reading nonverbal cues
- ☐ showing appropriate concern for others

Choose a skill from the list that you feel your children have yet to master or are ready to tackle. How might you introduce the topic at your next shared meal?

Think of ways you can model the desired skill and then think of gentle, fun, and accepting ways to introduce this behavior.

Exercise B: For All

Think about the last time you shared a meal with someone. Was it a routine meal or a special occasion? Where did you eat? What did you eat? What was the environment like? What did you talk about? Was the flow of communication easy, difficult, or somewhere in between? How could you tell how your companion was feeling—through words, body language, vocal inflection and tone, or some combination? Sit for a few moments and recall what the complete experience was like.

On a piece of paper or in a word-processing file, describe the parts of the interaction that were socially successful. For example, did you pick up on the fact that your companion was worried about something (even though she didn't say so) and ask her about it? Did you feel as though your companion understood exactly what you were saying?

Now describe the parts of the interaction that were socially awkward or unappealing. Were there times when you felt as though you had nothing to say? Were there uncomfortable silences? Did your companion behave in an obnoxious manner or eat self-consciously?

Finally, identify one social skill you would like to improve—whether listening more attentively, following nonverbal cues as you explain an idea, having plenty to talk about, sharing your feelings, or anything that comes to you. List some simple ways you might practice to improve this skill the next time.

Exercise C: For All

Who among your friends and acquaintances is the one person with whom you would most like to share a meal? What makes this person such a great mealtime companion? What social skills does this person have that you admire? Consider inviting this person to share meals with you on a regular basis.

Physical Development

Eating healthy doesn't take any more or less time. It's just choosing better.
—Michael Kirkbride

An important part of human development is physical development. The body is healthiest when we provide all the nutrients and exercise needed to function well. Tragically, in the United States today, the alarming incidence of obesity is signaling a serious problem in the way Americans view their physical health.

Data gathered by The Centers for Disease Control and Prevention (CDC) released in 2010 showed that more than 72 million Americans are obese, and that *zero* of our states have an obesity rate less than 15 percent (our national goal). The CDC also reports that 17 percent of children and adolescents between the ages of two and nineteen are obese—*tripling* from a generation ago. They further reported if a child is overweight, he is likely to suffer from more severe obesity as an adult. Addressing obesity and nutrition habits when children are young (and in need of nutritional guidance) is important because obesity is a major risk factor for many preventable diseases, including heart disease, diabetes, and some cancers.

The high incidence of obesity is directly tied to the fact that the average American meal fails to meet basic nutritional standards. People in the United States consume more processed foods per capita than do the people of any other country. We eat an alarming 40 percent of the world's frozen and pre-prepared meals, including soup. Most children don't meet the CDC's daily recommendations of two and a half to six and a half cups of fruits and vegetables and two to three ounces of whole grains. They consume too much salt and too many empty calories laden with fat and sugar. Clearly, there's work to do in helping the nation's children eat healthier.

During the years when I was raising my kids, I occasionally bought processed, frozen meals. Like so many parents, I was tempted by the promise of convenience and swayed by my kids' pleas for the fun, colorfully packaged Kid Cuisine meals. We discussed food selection together on a regular basis. We didn't always make the most nutritional choices as my kids reached their teen years, but we were generally successful. I believe that because of the many discussions we had, Jini is now in the habit of making healthy choices, such as frequently choosing a salad as an entrée. When John went away to college, he often made surprisingly healthy choices and learned more about what constitutes "whole foods." Today, he drinks a blended juice and vegetable drink for nutrition every day. On *rare* occasions, I still might make choices that include packaged or processed foods, but the majority of the time I focus my diet on leafy greens, fruits, whole grains, and sometimes indulge in a sweet treat. It turns out that as I was teaching my children, I was adopting more nutritious choices myself—first by habit, then by preference.

A difficult truth is that Americans are in the middle of a health crisis generated in part by chronically unhealthy eating habits. We eat for short-term convenience and quickly consume what is easily accessible rather than making food choices that bring us long-term nutritional benefits.

Many adults eat on the run or alone; therefore, many children eat meals without supervision or company. Children depend on adults to teach them positive eating habits and model healthy choices. A helpful starting point would be to simply talk about what you're eating. When parents aren't aware of their influence on children's nutritional choices, they inadvertently contribute to the obesity problem. If this pattern persists, America will continue this crisis generationally.

Certain factors seem to contribute to dietary composition in homes with teens, such as socioeconomic conditions and types of food that are available (due to cost or cultural norms), as well as parents' typical meal habits. Researchers at Project EAT, a program run by the School of Public Health at the University of Minnesota, performed a longitudinal study to determine if regular family meals (in this case, five or more family meals per week) helped with better nutrition. Nearly seven hundred children approximately twelve years of age took the surveys, which they repeated five years later. They found that although the frequency of family meals was down from 60 percent to 30 percent once the kids hit the age of seventeen, those who had maintained regular family meals during the five years had healthier diets and better patterns of eating compared to those teens who did not share regular family meals. Researcher Teri L. Burgess-Champoux concluded that although the majority of teens in the study still didn't meet national nutritional standards, having regular family meals during those transitional adolescent years did promote healthier eating. Another study conducted by the researchers at Project EAT was composed of 1,700 young adults around the ages of fifteen. Five years later, at age twenty, it showed that family meals appeared to have a positive impact on their diet quality. They consumed more fruit and green leafy vegetables and fewer soft drinks.

Another survey, this one from Baylor College of Medicine, found that grade school kids who ate with their parents were healthier and consumed more fruits and vegetables and less fat. Children in homes without regular family meal habits ate at least half of their meals watching television and tended to be overweight.

Parents may not serve the most nutritious meals 100 percent of the time, but dinner together gives parents a regular venue to talk about good nutrition, acceptable portion sizes, and the use of food as energy. Most importantly, according to Dr. Michael Rosenbaum, associate professor of clinical pediatrics and medicine at the New York Presbyterian Hospital at Columbia University, when parents select nutritious food in the presence of their children, it is a far more effective method than simply talking about abstract rules. Parents don't need to demonize fatty or sugary foods to teach that such foods are best eaten sparingly; they need only serve these foods in small quantities to send that message. Adults who demonstrate moderation, pleasure, and mindfulness when eating can help children build a healthy, lifelong relationship with food. This role modeling will help counteract the powerful media influence of unhealthy food products.

Eating with others, especially without outside distractions, also encourages both children and adults to slow their intake of food and become aware of what they're eating. Carl Honoré, in his book *In Praise of Slowness*, reports that eating slowly has the added benefit of allowing the brain to register that the stomach has received the food that it needs, thereby preventing the tendency to overeat.

A study published in *Psychological Science* suggests more support for culinary rituals. Researchers from the University of Minnesota in Minneapolis and Harvard University found that performing "ritualized gestures" may increase our ability to savor our food, increase its flavor, and make it more enjoyable because the ritual creates "involvement" in the food we are about to consume. This was true for a range of food from chocolate to baby carrots. Although the experiments these researchers used consisted of systematic gestures (such as knocking twice, taking a deep breath, and snapping fingers), this research has important implications that meal rituals can help support better nutrition.

Chef Jamie Oliver is a strong voice for food education and healthy habits in schools and in homes. He says, "Home needs to be the heart of passing on food culture." Oliver also offers some wonderful programs to get kids in the kitchen and give them hands-on cooking skills.

For children at various stages of development, preparing and sharing a meal with an adult offers other ways to develop physically. There are many opportunities in the kitchen for kids to practice fine and gross motor skills. For example, a toddler can practice dexterity at the dining table as he learns to handle his first cup or spoon. A young child can develop gross motor skills when placing a bowl of fruit on a table or helping a parent pour glasses of milk. Older children can assist preparing food in activities that require a bit more advanced skill, such as scrubbing and peeling vegetables, or stirring a pot of simmering spaghetti sauce on the stove, with adult supervision.

During my childhood, our parents did not formally teach the concepts of proper nutrition or the use of food as energy. Meals consisted of meat, potatoes, a vegetable (often corn, peas, or potatoes, or something now considered in the high-glycemic category), and dessert. In my family study, several of my siblings said growing up believing dessert should be part of every dinner contributed to their desire for sweets. The only direction our parents gave us regarding portion control was to eat everything we were served. This rule was not uncommon among parents who had lived through a severe economic depression.

I grew up realizing my parents' standards were an expression of their love, as well as their assurance that their offspring would not go hungry. Loving or not, the rules are probably part of the reason many of us sometimes struggle with weight management and portion control. Fortunately, this has eased over time as we have educated ourselves and improved our habits.

Good eating habits do not come naturally in a marketplace that offers a wide variety of cheap, easily accessible, and unhealthy food. It is genuinely difficult to separate clutter and hype from clear and accurate information. Ideally, everyone would prepare home-cooked meals using fresh, local ingredients. But that ideal is a long way off for many. It is unrealistic (and emotionally unhealthy) to think you always need to achieve perfection, but we can do better. Better is a fine place to start. If we commit to improving one thing about the food we eat and share with others, we can begin to make a difference in our physical development. Once we have seen improvement in one area, we can move on to another aspect of our eating habits.

Healthy eating benefits not only the body but ecological systems too. Author Barbara Kingsolver states, "The average food item on a U.S. grocery shelf has traveled farther than most families go on their annual vacations." Some food production and distribution practices are quite detrimental to natural resources. But consumers can directly influence these practices through the choices they make when they purchase food.

Popular food journalist Mark Bittman suggests we come to our senses about what we're choosing to eat, and watch over time as those choices turn into a way of life. He defines his recommendations of "eating sanely" as eating from local sources, eating far less meat and more protein-rich legumes than we currently consume, choosing whole grains over refined carbohydrates, cutting out as much junk and processed food as possible, and zeroing in on green, leafy plants. Bittman urges, "Eat all the plants you can manage. Literally. Gorge on them."

When we pay attention to the types of foods we eat and where this food is coming from, we get an added benefit from our shared-meal ritual: in caring for each other, we are also taking care of Mother Earth.

Exercise: Have Your Cauliflower and Eat It Too

Physical development is not about depriving yourself of delicious foods. Some of the most delicious foods are right under your nose, waiting to be noticed and appreciated.

Exercise A: For All

Keep a journal of the kinds of foods you eat for a month. Let go of any shame or guilt you might feel; just list the foods you've been eating. At the end of your month, describe how you think your diet is benefitting or detracting from your physical development. Write this description in the most detached and clinical way you can.

If you are interested in examining the specifics of your diet, consider using a site like http://nutritiondata.self.com/ which offers a variety of tools that allow you to compare foods, search nutrients, and track your diet using bar graphs and pie charts to display the percentages of fats, protein, carbohydrates, and calories you are eating daily.

After identifying what you currently eat, make a list of foods in your journal that taste especially good to you and are also good for your body. Make this list as long as you can, expand it, and write comments about the foods.

Exercise B: For Parents of Young Children

At the dinner table, start a running conversation about food. For example, if you are a mother, you might start by commenting on something that tastes delicious to you: "Mmmm, I love broccoli, especially when Dad cooks it for us in the steam basket." Wait for your children to continue the conversation or prompt them to reveal what they like about the meal you're eating. Two minutes per meal is ample time to spend talking about food—just long enough to help your children become aware of what they're putting in their mouths. As the dialogue progresses over time, talk about which foods are the best fuel for our bodies (vegetables, fruit, healthy oils like olive and canola, whole grains), which foods build and repair the body (lean meats and other proteins, dairy products), and which foods are less beneficial as fuel and "building materials" (highly refined grains, sugar-filled, processed foods).

Exercise C: For Parents of Older Children

As with young children, start a running conversation about food at the family table. Ask older children to identify their favorite foods, both in the meal you are eating and in general. You might ask fun, hypothetical questions such as, "If you could eat only three foods for the rest of your life, which three would you choose?" Allow the children to answer in whatever way they like without judging their answers. If you notice something concerning—such as all their favorite foods are chock-full of sugar and fat—wait until the next meal and talk about how the body uses the nutrients we feed it. Ask the children to pay attention to how their bodies feel thirty minutes after they eat a sugary or fat-filled snack. Don't spend too much time at each meal talking about food and nutrition, but if your children show interest in the topics, help them to find related library books and websites to increase their knowledge.

Psychological Development

What unites us as human beings is an urge for happiness, which at heart is a yearning for union.
—Sharon Salzberg

Sharing meals yields an abundance of psychological benefits for people of all ages. Psychologically healthy people have stable self-esteem and positive personal identity.

Psychological health in young children largely depends on feelings of safety and security. Children need routines and repetition of activities that promise predictable outcomes to establish these feelings. My childhood household bustled with the activity of eleven children; thankfully, my parents were acutely aware of the need for order and routine. A family meal ritual was a highlight of that structure. I always knew that despite any incidental troubles I might be feeling throughout my day, the warmth of a family meal would help me to feel better.

Family therapist Ellyn Satter, author of *Child of Mine: Feeding with Love and Good Sense,* believes a household dynamic in which children feel secure and loved needs to happen by intent. The ritual of sharing meals sends a specific message confirming the parent's overall commitment to the child's well-being. It's a small action that speaks volumes about the mind-set and priorities of the parent. As I was raising Jini and John, I recall on some occasions getting a halfhearted greeting after they arrived home from school. Soon after, they would dependably call out, "What's for dinner?" That call was my assurance that keeping a meal ritual was a wise activity. Sometimes they chose to reveal if something was bothering them, and sometimes they didn't. I believe just knowing our family would be gathering around the dinner table gave them comfort.

A study published in the *Journal of Epidemiology and Community Health* found a trend in mental health benefits for children who regularly shared meals with their family. Those who shared meals six or more times a week exhibited better overall mental health and sought counseling less often than those who had fewer than five meals together a week. These frequent diners also spent time in other activities with their families. My experience showed it was fairly easy to get my children to do other activities with me—whether running an errand, shopping for a friend's birthday gift, or visiting a neighbor—because they already had experienced togetherness of our family meals. In a sense, our meals primed them for our other activities.

Sharing meals can also help your children have better relationships with their friends, according to data gathered at Cincinnati Children's Hospital Medical Center. I find both of my children are empathic and loyal friends. I have often credited those qualities to the supportive conversations we had at the dinner table, which extended to their relationships outside our home. As an adult, I find that meals I share with my friends only further cement the bonds of friendship we have with one another.

Some families have more than their share of domestic problems, including substance or alcohol abuse in the home. A 1987 study performed by psychiatrist Steven J. Wolin and his colleagues examined the stabilizing effects of rituals in alcoholic homes, including eating dinner together. The study showed that in those alcoholic homes where rituals were held, fewer children became alcoholics as adults, concluding that rituals offer a stabilizing effect and bring unity to a family, even those living in distressed environments. This is compelling evidence to illustrate the stability sharing meals with your family provides.

Today's children deal with significantly more complex emotional issues than generations past. The youngest of today's youth are expected to live up to the pressures of intense academic competition, heinously cluttered schedules, and a saturated media culture full of unrealistic images. It is pressure I couldn't have imagined during my relatively modest childhood in the sixties. Add to this a host of modern social pressures—racism, school bullying, and pressure to become sexually active at ages younger than ever—and our children become even more vulnerable. Sharing meals with your family won't be a cure-all for all of the instability that's present in our world, but I believe having such a forum does allow the opportunity for family members to meaningfully watch over one another.

Children of all ages can discover their personality preferences—who they are and who they are not—through dialogue at the family table. Systems of communication that are considered "open"—that is, characterized by the freedom to talk about a variety of topics with an emphasis on building self-worth—encourage the development of a healthy identity.

In particular, teenagers (who often find unique ways to express their personalities) can develop their identities through food choices and preferences. As my daughter reached her late teens, she developed a liking for soy milk and offered information at the dinner table about soy milk versus milk from cows.

A recent study by CASA reveals correlations between infrequent family dining and teenagers' ability to access marijuana and prescription drugs: "Compared to teens who have five to seven family dinners per week, those who have fewer than three family dinners per week are more than twice as likely to say they can get marijuana in an hour, and one and a half times likelier to say they can get prescription drugs (to get high) in an hour," the study said.

Unhealthy eating behaviors often surface during adolescence in both boys and girls. Left to their own devices, teenagers may eat sporadically or make poor food choices based on convenience, lack of education about nutritional foods, or laziness. Some will develop serious eating disorders, such as bulimia or anorexia nervosa. As reported by the National Eating Disorders Association (NEDA), approximately ten million women or girls and one million men or boys across the country suffer from eating disorders. Causes include emotional issues influenced by the media's portrayal of unsafe body images. Parents can help teenagers to eat better and help protect them from these destructive disorders by hosting family meals.

When my teenage daughter went through a phase of closely examining what she would eat because she perceived everything made her "fat," I was concerned. In deciding how to respond, I asked for her increased help planning meals. After several days of prodding, I finally suggested we make a homemade pizza (a family favorite), hoping to get her attention. This prompted a conversation about her "fat" concerns, because in the past we had sometimes used a fair amount of cheese on our pizza. She suggested we use less cheese and more olives and mushrooms to make the pizza less heavy. During that year, she became more involved in menu planning and enjoyed experimenting with ingredients. I think this period of time helped to distract her from her concerns about body image and instead gave her a productive sense of control over what she was eating. In her case, it helped to diffuse the anxiety she was having. I was very lucky that she didn't respond to being "fat-obsessed" in a self-destructive way. Today, she's probably the most educated person in our family about moderate and healthy eating habits. She still enjoys splurging now and again, but without guilt or signs of obsession.

Not every teenager will react with the same openness, but a shared-meal ritual offers a position for modeling portion control, the ability to witness cues a teen may be sending about their relationship with food, and an opportunity to address concerns about body image. Studies show families who dine together at least three to four meals a week have less disordered eating. So there is an apparent payoff in making the investment in shared meals to ward off eating disorders.

Research conducted by the University of Minnesota's Project EAT found that routine family meals may provide some emotional protection for adolescents, especially females, who seem to be slightly more affected by family meal experiences versus their male counterparts. This study was unique in that it separated the factor of existing "family connectedness," suggesting that the benefit of family meals for teens is "above and beyond their general sense of connection" with their families.

Even though some research suggests girls may be experiencing even more benefit than boys from a shared family meal, adolescent boys can build emotional connections through interactions at shared meals. Family therapist and social philosopher Michael Gurian, who has written extensively about the development of adolescent boys, warns that young males start looking away from the family during their middle teen years. He says it's the routines in the household that help a boy feel stable and offers that "clan activity" could help keep a young man from seeking emotional needs away from home.

Like girls, adolescent boys also experience changes in their bodies, including overt changes in height, weight, and voice. Bursts of testosterone provide increased energy. I recall a steady buzz of energy emanating from my son at our dining table during his early teen years, and it surely captured my attention. The dining table offers an opportunity for a parent to observe these hormonal changes in a son (or daughter) and discuss ways to use this energy positively— for example, through sports or creative arts. A family meal not only provides a place for meaningful interaction for our sons, but it's also a safe place where they can learn to express a wide range of emotions (tenderness, sensitivity, empathy), something not every young male in American society is accustomed, or encouraged, to do.

Gurian stresses the importance of ritualistic activity in a family: "Protect your family rituals like they are gold." He recommends having at least one meal together a day and asks caregivers to strongly consider gathering over a meal a high priority over other activities.

In light of the information I've shared, we can see that sharing meals can be a safeguard from potential psychological health problems in children.

Although psychological health is especially important for growing children, sharing meals also significantly impacts adult emotional health. When I was raising my children, knowing that I contributed to their well-being by maintaining a family meal ritual gave me contentment that continues to this day. Regularly interacting with my children during our family meals significantly lowered my anxiety. The merry-go-round of activities halted at least once a day, allowing me to be present with my kids in real time and reminding us all to be free from distractions and in the moment with each other.

The 2005 CASA report supports my own experience; it found families who share dinners more frequently (at least five dinners per week) have less stress, and that means everyone, including the adults, copes better and experiences more joy.

At a workshop I recently attended with about fifty other women, we discussed values and setting priorities. The conversation turned to lessons learned in the past year. One woman offered that she had been laid off from her job, cancelled the vacation abroad she had been planning for years, and was facing foreclosure on her house. But despite these tumultuous events, her biggest regret was being so distracted from the events of her life that she and her son (on his summer break from college) did not share as many meals together, a ritual they had enjoyed for years. She lamented how much she had missed their time in the kitchen preparing food, the laughter, and "everything else that goes along with that kind of time together." She and her son decided nothing would get in the way on future visits.

Notable psychologist and author Frederic Hudson says our lives are marked by constant change. Unfortunately, American culture doesn't always respond well to change. Instead of embracing the process, we react by trying to remove the uncertainty it presents us. Family meals are a casualty of dealing with an ever-changing environment. We resort to insulating ourselves in personal concerns, and also spending our energy acquiring material things, leaving us absent of the important link between ourselves and societal health. This is unfortunate because when we allow for this link to be weakened, we are losing a precious opportunity to promote a healthy culture.

Hudson argues we're not actively engaged in activities of renewal that allow us to attend to "body, mind, and spirit." Hudson's ten qualities of self-renewal include being value driven, making decisions allowing us to live a reasonably paced life, adapting to change by evaluating and revising areas that are not working, and living with a consciousness of today and wonder about tomorrow. Adults who lead the way in a shared-meal practice are living in alignment with Hudson's ideals.

Hudson believes leadership in the twenty-first century will come from those "who are ready to do more with their lives than merely succeed and consume." I like to think of this century as a time to recognize both shared responsibility and shared opportunity.

A particular problem in our American society is when adults age, they sometimes feel cast aside in a society that glorifies youth. Older people may live alone, suffer failing health, and inevitably begin to lose friends and family members to illness. These circumstances lead to isolation, which causes anxiety and depression. Loss of appetite is one of the by-products of depression. When senior members of our communities are not meeting basic nutritional needs, the results are devastating. Therefore, it's literally vital to their health that we purposefully share meals with them.

Exercise: Polishing the Apple

Psychological well-being is a complex issue that affects us throughout our life span and is important at every age. Reflect upon what you have just read about positive psychological health and use these simple exercises to stimulate positive thinking and behaviors.

Exercise A: For Parents

Bolster your child's or teenager's self-esteem by asking open-ended questions at the table. For example, rather than asking, "Did you have a good day?" which can be answered yes or no, ask, "What did you do today?" Listen to your child's answers with an open mind. If you sense that she is saying something to get a particular reaction from you, use an active listening technique and repeat back what was said for clarity. For example, say, "So, you're saying you think you should be able to stay out as late as Sasha, because you're the same age?" Then, express yourself in terms of your own viewpoint. Rather than saying, "That's a silly request," say, "What concerns me about that idea is . . ."

It is inevitable that when you talk with your child or teenager at the table, he will say something sensational. When this happens, try this technique: pause to think of something you admire about your child or teenager. If you can, share it with him right at that moment.

Exercise B: For All

Is self-renewal automatic for you at this point in your life? Or do you sometimes tip into self-defeat? Wherever your answer falls on the renewal-defeat continuum, you have something in common with the rest of us: we can all improve one step at a time. Self-renewal is a skill, so it can be learned. Below are some ideas for practicing it.

From the list below, choose one activity that you know you can do right now (or create your own) and plan to put it into practice soon. How about today?

To practice being motivated by values, you can:
- Eat something that is both nutritious and delicious at every meal.
- Decide to stop eating in your car or at your desk.
- Show a loved one you are thinking of him by preparing a favorite meal or dish.
- Make a dish you have been craving or have wanted to make for a long time.

To practice being connected to the world, you can:
- Donate food to a local food bank.
- Attend a meal at a club you belong to, a charity fundraiser, or your place of worship.
- Volunteer to serve food at a local soup kitchen on a day other than Thanksgiving or Christmas.
- Volunteer to share meals with senior citizens at an assisted-living center, a nursing home, a hospital, or a hospice facility.

To practice being future oriented, you can:
- Plan your next meal, making it as simple as it needs to be for your comfort, shop for the necessary groceries, and prepare and enjoy the meal with good company.
- Organize a potluck meal with friends or family members to celebrate a special occasion.
- Plan with friends or family members to share a meal once a week, once a month, or once every two months.

Part B

Creative Development

Creativity is inventing, experimenting, growing, taking risks, breaking rules, making mistakes, and having fun.
—Mary Lou Cook

Children and adults alike can build creative skills when preparing meals. Building creativity in the kitchen can also enhance creative ability in other areas such as fine arts and design. In my study, I asked my siblings to discuss whether sharing family meals had fostered their creative skills. Several mentioned skills they developed as a result of our family meal ritual.

Debra, Edith, and Rose said they learned creativity with balancing spices, such as finding the right blend of seasoning for a pot of homemade soup. Debra felt our family meals taught her to prepare complex meals for large groups of people with ease. Barb agreed, noting she later used those skills as owner/chef at her New Hampshire bed-and-breakfast. Both learned to make complete last-minute meals from limited pantry staples. Edith mentioned our home meals sparked her imagination: she remembered arranging mashed sweet potatoes shaped as flower petals around a ham and recalled our father's compliments for her artistry. Rose learned to inject some fun by playing with the appearance of foods—such as green eggs and ham she served her children.

They also described other creative abilities they honed not directly related to preparing food. Barb said sharing meals helped her learn to be distinctive and develop appropriate timing when chiming into conversation, as well as how to use creative storytelling in her short story writing. Rose remembers frequent dinnertime conversations supporting our interest in music and singing in three-part harmony with her sisters while drying dishes. I fondly recall my father's humorous request to speed along the cleanup process. He'd offer with a wink, "Can you girls sing a faster song?"

Several of my brothers said sharing meals helped to develop a creative approach to life, including delivering a joke with precision and using humor in difficult situations. Ned told me watching our parents prepare meals influenced him to experiment with ingredients. He also shared that when raising his daughters, he used improvisational skills to repair a recipe glitch. Creative lessons I've learned through meal activities have had an impact on me in effective time management, problem solving, and an appreciation for design.

These comments remind me of similar remarks made by chefs Rachael Ray and Jamie Oliver who promote the idea of adults and children working together in the kitchen. Certainly there is widespread agreement among all chefs that cooking is an art providing limitless opportunities for creativity in recipes, food combinations, techniques, and presentation.

Exercise: Icing on the Cake

When it comes to sharing meals, there are so many ways to be creative the list seems endless. Here are a few suggestions to get you started in making your own list. Continue it by writing your ideas on a separate sheet of paper or in a word-processing file.

Invite children and adults to create placemats, name placeholders for guests, or other table decorations.

Create drawings or other artwork to decorate your dining area.

Next time you are making a dish you have made before, change one or two ingredients and see how it turns out.

Take children to a paint-your-own ceramics store where they can create personalized platters, plates, bowls, mugs, napkin holders, salt and pepper shakers, or candle holders.

Experiment with cooking simple ethnic dishes and having friends or family members create table decorations to go with the meal.

Allow one or two older children to lead the family through the planning and preparation of a dish or a whole meal.

Design a birthday tablecloth for the guest of honor. Do this by asking everyone to sign a white tablecloth in colored marker. Each year, bring out the tablecloth for new comments to be added.

Create a "favorite things" table for someone celebrating a birthday or achievement. The table can be filled with items to represent the favorite things of this person and celebrate the event.

Host a "backward night" for neighbors and serve dessert first and salad last.

Have a picnic in your living room.

Plan a theme night in which the meal, music, and clothing are coordinated.

Cultural and Ethnic Development

The duty of a good cuisinier is to transmit to the next generation everything he has learned and experienced.
—Fernand Point

Rutgers University anthropologist Robin Fox says, "A meal is about civilizing children. It's about teaching them to be a member of their culture." She quips, "If it were just about food, we would squirt it into their mouths with a tube." Naturally, none of us is born knowing our cultural identity. We first learn about culture from our earliest years in the home. As we mature, we grow to understand what is generally accepted as family, then community, and ultimately, national culture. In the earliest research on the benefits of sharing meals, sociologists identified the family unit as "the chief culture-transmitting agency in our society." When meal rituals are present, consider the powerful impact on family and American culture. When they're not, it's a lost opportunity.

A mix of ethnic backgrounds is something that makes America such a wonderfully dynamic place to live. It's important to preserve our ethnic histories so they can enrich our overall culture. When family members prepare meals together, recipes and other traditions that represent each family's unique identity are passed to the next generation.

In my study of family meals, each of my siblings felt our mother's Italian ethnicity was prevalent in the family recipes and in the behaviors of our Italian relatives. Habits such as my maternal grandfather drinking wine at meals and giving several children a sip (the amount varying according to the child's age) were a cultural norm for our family. Through the years my older sisters—who along with our mother were primarily responsible for planning, preparing, and serving each meal—naturally developed a repertoire that honored Italian traditions.

Many of us have fond memories of enjoying elaborate meals with traditional Italian desserts such as Easter ricotta pie. Several siblings remember Italian words being used such as *mangia* (eat), and there was a prominent feeling that Italians take pride in making recipes from scratch. We carefully guarded our mother's recipes until passing them to our own children. As adults, we each maintain bragging rights over dishes our parents taught us to make.

Mealtime conversation is another major way to transmit culture. Discussions allow a family to explore similarities and unique qualities of each member's personality. Bossard said conversation around the table is much like a "university seminar on family culture, continuing over a number of semesters." Storytelling—a powerful way to communicate and especially effective in exploring cultural identity—should be encouraged during a family meal. Stories about ancestors surface naturally at the table, and richly detailed stories (sometimes humorously embellished, as was the case during my childhood) help everyone better understand the larger cultural group to which they belong.

Knowledge of family history also plays an important role in helping children handle the stress of everyday life. Graduate research student Amber Lazarus studied this phenomenon among children living in New York City before and after the terrorist attacks of September 11, 2001. Lazarus found that the children's strong sense of the family unit provided a "consistent protective factor" in response to stress. Although her study was small (twenty-one families), her findings implied that parents who share family stories with their children may be helping them to withstand crisis.

Older members of a family are invaluable sources of information about the family's history. Many older people have a strong interest in securing their legacy by sharing words of wisdom, knowledge, and advice with younger generations. Children are naturally interested in stories about people who came before them. Stories shared at the table can help grandparents and grandchildren do what author Mary Pipher refers to as "grow our souls together," sacred bonding between these two generations.

I remember having Sunday morning breakfasts with my kids and their paternal grandparents, Jerry and Pat. Jerry would share stories about his childhood, including how his mother pickled cucumbers and made jam from locally grown fruits. When we visited Oregon, my kids would see the jars neatly stored in the garage and make a selection.

I recall my mother telling the story that she and her sister were often sent to their backyard to catch a live chicken for dinner. This was a normal part of life in their family. We were shocked to learn they didn't get their chicken at the local Stop & Shop.

My father told charming stories over dinner. One was his enduring memory of the day he learned to walk. He bragged to us that he realized if he pretended he couldn't walk for a while, he would continue to be carried around. He would also cheerfully recount the details about the day he was born. He cleverly wove these stories into mealtime conversations. And it was his storytelling of historical world events that helped us understand our place in American culture.

Pipher reminds us that, "Our elders have special needs and special gifts. If we will slow down and listen, we can learn from the old." Older family members recall when society emphasized "we" rather than "me." I often hear soulful stories from people in their senior years about times they worked through very trying situations (such as settling in America after immigrating through Ellis Island and what daily life was like during the Great Depression) in ways that honored their family's culture.

Surely, there is plenty of opportunity to develop cultural and ethnic identity across multiple generations through conversations at shared meals.

Exercise: Peas in a Pod

Take a moment to think about which characteristics of your culture you most relate to and ways you can express your culture through shared-meal activities.

Here are a few to get you started:

Identify a dish you enjoyed as a child but have never made or find a recipe that has been passed along from an earlier generation. If you haven't prepared and shared this dish (or if it's been a while), plan when you will make it. If possible, have a family member from another generation help.

Write a journal entry, have a discussion with a family member, or start a table conversation about symbolism that certain dishes carry for you.

Ask older members of your family about dishes they enjoyed as children. Why did they like the dishes then? Do they like them still? Do they know how to make them? Can they teach them to you?

Invite older members in your family to share a meal with you. During the meal, ask questions such as, "What has been your favorite place to live and why?" and "What has been one of the happiest moments of your life?"

Ask the oldest persons at the table to describe the style of dancing that was popular when they were young or to share who their favorite musical entertainers were when they were your age.

Take a field trip to a nearby grocery store that specializes in foods of a certain ethnicity (such as Indian). Pick up some *masala* for a traditional Indian dish. Find a local restaurant that serves authentic native dishes (such as a Chinese meal of *dim sum* or *hotpot*).

Academic Development

Learning is a treasure that will follow its owner everywhere.
—Chinese proverb

When we think of academic development, we think first of children. However, whether attending college, taking training or technical courses, or simply being dedicated to lifelong learning, adults are often students too. The practice of sharing meals affects academic development both directly and indirectly. Showing interest in someone's academic pursuits during a shared meal sets a tone of concern. The support I received when sharing meals with others while preparing my master's thesis was very helpful.

Available research on the topic of academic development and sharing meals correlates most strongly with children and adolescents. Children increase their vocabulary (especially in their early years) through activities that encourage speaking, asking questions, and listening. Conversations over a meal provide a natural forum to help build literacy in children. A Harvard study agreed that "family meals promote language development even more than does family story reading."

If parents or caregivers want to seize teachable moments that pop up at the dining table, they can introduce food names and other new words that allow children to practice language in a safe environment. A parent might say, "Look at this skinny spaghetti—it's called *cappellini*." Or, instead of saying the more common phrase, "Isn't it *yummy*?" a parent could offer a more sophisticated word such as, "Isn't it *scrumptious*?" Diane E. Beals, assistant professor of education at Washington University, describes this strategy to expand vocabulary, along with engaging your child in extended conversation on any topic, as a way to boost critical thinking skills. As was the case with my chatty kids, it's a lot of fun to see what words you each can find to describe the taste or appearance of food.

Direct educational benefits are available when children of any age help prepare and serve food. As mentioned earlier, gross and fine motor skills can grow when a child is learning to lift a melon onto a counter or learning the right amount of pressure to apply when poking toothpicks into strawberries. A young child can practice learning numbers by counting out six eggs to help his father prepare a small group breakfast. Seriating skills (following a series or sequence of directions) can be practiced when reading simple recipes. I gave my daughter a children's cookbook when she was twelve; it became a favorite of hers, and we still use the banana bread recipe included in this book. With my kids, I found plenty of safe and fun opportunities, such as peeling bananas, adding cherry tomatoes to a salad, or placing rounds of mozzarella on a pizza shell. Even the youngest of children can get involved fetching measuring spoons or keeping track of how many stirs they gave the mashed potatoes.

At a slightly older age, children might benefit from learning about where a certain food is grown. After we finished a bowl of miso soup, I pointed out to a friend's grandchild where Japan was located on a Google map. Helping to educate children about food origin allows them to understand that food type and eating habits of various cultures depends on geographical location; not all foods are available everywhere, and food doesn't sprout in a brightly colored package in the frozen-food section of the supermarket. Preteens and older adolescents who like the taste of ethnic foods can learn to make their favorite dishes for the rest of the family and share other information about the country of origin too.

There are learning opportunities that naturally surface in the kitchen (especially in science and math) and can be explored while you're having fun. Children are exposed to fascinating chemistry lessons when preparing food. For example, you might explain why onions can cause people to cry or why it's important to add baking soda to cake recipes.

For all children, improvising solutions to unexpected situations when preparing or serving food will improve problem-solving skills. Also, by helping prepare food, picky eaters will learn about unfamiliar food items. Expose kids to new foods without assuming they'll refuse them because they are foreign to what is normally served. Sometimes you may be right, and your child will reject something new—but not always. I remember placing a small assortment of olives on the table nearby my son on different occasions. The first time or two, he ignored the olives. However, at a future meal I noticed him moving around the different shapes with a fork. Soon after, he tried a kalamata olive and discovered he liked it.

A shared-meal practice also creates opportunities for impromptu cooking guidance between older and younger generations. Grandparents may have anecdotal information about ways to prepare food that children will not find in a cookbook. My mother showed me how to manipulate buttercream frosting with a spoon in a way that I have not seen since. When I was a little older, she showed me how to use a sausage grinder and a hand-cranked ice cream maker.

Chopping carrots or celery by hand allows us to feel the different textures of food, which is something less obvious when using an electric chopper or food processor. Children can learn as they mature what food they'll work with by hand versus what modern technology they'll choose.

A big bonus in sharing meals routinely with your teens is that it will help them get better grades in school. Several reports have been issued by CASA promoting family meal rituals. One CASA report showed that teens who sit down for dinner with their families five or more times during the week are "almost twice as likely to receive As in school compared to teens who have dinner with their families two or fewer times a week." Similarly, another CASA report stated that teens who have dinner with their families once every day are nearly 40 percent likelier to say they receive mostly As and Bs in school compared to those teens who had dinner twice or less per week with their families. According to a later CASA study, when shared meals don't happen regularly (fewer than three family dinners per week), kids are "one and a half times likelier to report getting mostly Cs or lower grades in school."

As CASA's name suggests (National Center on Addiction and Substance Abuse), of primary concern to their research are substance abuse risk factors and identifying and mitigating those risks. They believe parental engagement is closely connected to substance abuse risk, and they strongly recommend parents and teens get this engagement through frequently shared meals. CASA reports the more often kids share meals with their parents, the less likely they are to abuse substances; consequently, these kids achieve better academic performance.

Exercise: Cream of the Crop

Adapt any of the shared-meal activities below to make them age appropriate for your children or your adult friends or family members. On a separate sheet of paper, or in a word-processing file, list the top five ideas you would like to try. Add a few original ideas of your own if you feel inspired. Refer to this list until you've crossed off each item.

At the dinner table, ask fellow diners who are students (of any age) to talk about their favorite academic subjects or classes. Ask them if they'd like to volunteer to describe something new they learned in their studies or reading.

Describe briefly your three all-time favorite books, explaining why you like each one. Ask your fellow diners to do the same.

Keep a small bowl on the table that contains words with simple definitions written on small pieces of paper. At mealtime, ask someone at the table to select a word and talk about its meaning or definition or use it in a sentence.

Ask volunteers to research food trivia facts about menu items in advance of that day's meal. (One source of these facts is the website http://www.foodreference.com.) For example, if you are making coleslaw, someone might look up which states lead in the production of cabbage (answer: California, followed by New York). The volunteers can share their trivia questions and answers at the start of the meal.

Watch online videos about the science of cooking and baking, such as those featuring Alton Brown, a food scientist and the host of *Good Eats*. The videos are available at http://www.foodnetwork.com/good-eats.

Go around the table and recite phrases that describe food or the act of eating in some way, such as, "This dress you're wearing shows you have good taste," "He's the top banana," or "My teacher, Ms. Clark, is a good egg." See how many examples you can find in everyday language.

Read a biography of a famous chef, such as Mario Batali; select and cook a dish from one of his cookbooks.

Describe to the youngest of your dining companions how kitchen technology has changed in recent years. Offer the story of a family member who would make bread from scratch, kneading the dough by hand. Explain that today some bakers would use a food processor for this task.

Together, review educational books on science and food. Explore various cooking methods mentioned in these books. For example, learn the differences between braising and searing. Try *I'm Just Here for the Food: Food + Heat = Cooking* by Alton Brown (New York: Stewart, Tabori and Chang, 2006).

Teach someone who is completely new to the kitchen the basics of how to read and follow a simple recipe, step-by-step.

Use online tools to help you grow an indoor garden. See http://tlc. howstuffworks.com/home/how-to-grow-your-own-indoor-herb-garden.htm.

Spiritual Development

The garden suggests there might be a place where we can meet nature halfway.
—Michael Pollan

Unfortunately, many Americans are allowing the shared-meal ritual and its many benefits to disappear. This implies we may not understand our own spiritual needs very well.

No matter what specific God you believe in (if you believe in a god at all), when people share healthful food together, they are making contact with nature and spiritual elements in their world. Because food is derived from the earth, and because we actually ingest it, it nurtures us from the inside of our souls, outward to our physical beings. Food is one of the earth's most fundamental gifts, rich with color and texture, representative of the colors of our lives.

When I eat whole foods, my sensory perception of my entire eating experience is elevated. I feel a difference in my well-being when eating a colorful heirloom tomato with fresh mozzarella and freshly picked basil leaves versus a heavily processed frozen meal in a box from the microwave. There's a dramatic shift in my outlook on life itself when I take care of myself by eating real food. I think to myself, "There's nothing like the real thing."

It's exciting for adults and children who participate in cooking whole foods to learn about the harvesting and distribution of that food and to see its journey from a garden or farm to a dinner plate.

When we eat in a rush or without mindfulness, we lose touch with food's spiritual significance. Taking the time to prepare and eat meals with others respects the natural availability of food. When we pick, clean, and cook ingredients, we are keeping ourselves humbly connected to the earth.

Important education to promote the consumption of whole foods is going on throughout the country, including work by chef and organic food activist Alice Waters. She is a veteran in helping us to understand the link between food and spiritual connection. She's hard at work with programs such as the *Edible Schoolyard* to raise children's awareness of the link between growing food and nurturing ourselves.

Author of *Cooked,* as well as other important books about food and agriculture, Michael Pollan suggests we can gain a "deeper understanding of the natural world" by spending time cooking in our kitchens.

Many people practice a ritual (religious or otherwise) of saying "grace" before meals, which recognizes that having food, in and of itself, is a blessing. For those of us who have full cupboards, we can honor our good fortune by sharing this food with people we love. During this time together, we can thoughtfully consider what the act of sharing food means.

Some people like to offer an informal blessing, such as the one my dear friend Angela created. She offers this simple blessing at the beginning of many shared meals in her home:

> To my family and friends
> Who are here tonight
> Gathered at this table
> You're the stars shining bright
> In the sky of my life
> Sparkling above
> Bringing me joy
> And so much love.
> Let us share this meal,
> Drink this wine,
> And I'll cherish this moment
> Until the end of time.
> ("Cheers!" or "Salute!")

Regularly sharing meals with others creates an important ritual. According to author Barbara Biziou, a ritual "conveys an act in which we literally join the metaphysical with the physical as a means of calling Spirit into our material lives." She says that by creating a ritual "we actively participate in our own development." Creating rituals (such as eating daily with your loved ones) promotes unity and a collective meaning for those involved.

Americans have grown accustomed to ritualistic-type activities. Many of us begin each workday by reading the morning news online while drinking a cup of coffee. We turn on the radio while we're stuck in traffic. We light candles in church in memory of loved ones. Some of these activities are repetitive habits set into our lifestyles, and others are cultural norms. Biziou says what makes a ritual powerful is that it carries personal meaning. If it doesn't, it won't be effective. Creating a shared-meal ritual can provide deep personal meaning when it is designed in ways special to that family. Regularly enjoying a shared-meal ritual offers spiritual benefits far beyond the act of cooking and eating.

My brother Tim described our childhood family meals as being similar to "communion," saying, "It wasn't vocalized, but it's the same thing as church." My brother Ned had a similar perspective; to him, spirituality is "making the best of what you have today, because you don't know what's going to happen tomorrow." He focuses on being present in the moment when sharing a meal with someone.

People often experience increasing connection to spirituality as they age. Rituals become more important to older members of the family as a way to feel stability. Sharing meals with an older relative or friend can lead to eye-opening conversations about the growing nature of spirituality over a lifetime.

Children who regularly eat with their grandparents often feel a sacred connection. Many young children say their grandparents have a special way of making an event magical. As author Mary Pipher says, "Small acts become ceremonial." My kids were fortunate to share many meals with their grandparents, aunts, and uncles over the years, and they have often commented it gave them a special feeling of unity about our family.

Exercise: Feeding the Soul

Exercise A: For All

What are some of your favorite rituals involving food? Do certain foods and their preparation hold a special place for you in a spiritual or religious tradition? Do you prepare certain foods in specific ways on religious or secular holidays? Do you eat certain foods only in certain settings or at certain times of the year? If possible, describe one of your food rituals to someone with whom you feel emotionally secure and invite that person to reciprocate. What does this ritual mean to you? How does it feed your spiritual self? Is it already part of a shared-meal routine? If not, how could you incorporate it into a shared-meal routine?

Exercise B: For Parents

If you live in an urban area and have young children, talk with them to gauge how much they know about where food comes from. You might do this while you are eating by saying, "I love carrots. Do you know of one place where carrots grow?" Choose your next step based on the depth of the children's knowledge.

For children who seem unsure about the origins of the foods they eat, discuss one food per meal and answer any questions they have.

For children who are more knowledgeable, consider organizing a visit to a family farm where food is grown; enjoy picking strawberries or other fruits and vegetables together. This is a field trip almost any child would enjoy.

If you have older children, find out together if your city has a community garden and explore membership.

Step 3

Making Room in Your Life for Shared Meals

To put the world in order, we must first put the nation in order; to put the nation in order, we must put the family in order; to put the family in order, we must cultivate our personal life; and to cultivate our personal life, we must first set our hearts right.
—Confucius

My daughter has a bumper sticker on her car declaring, "Change happens at the speed of thought." I like this quotation because it reminds me that I don't need to wait for the perfect time to change. I won't promise myself, "As soon as I do this, then . . ." I have the personal authority to start making changes now. We each have the same authority.

In current American culture, many of us are caught in a cycle of working, collapsing, consuming, and then repeating the process the next day at the sound of the alarm clock. We often feel lonely and disconnected, rarely slowing down to connect even with those closest to us. We live to accomplish short-term goals, careening through tasks and barreling through personal agendas. Merely squeezing in a moment here and there for relaxation (or, more likely, recovery) doesn't naturally afford the mental space to consider sharing a meal.

Our relationship with food has changed. It doesn't hold the same importance of pleasure and sociability for us anymore. There are many items on the menus of our lives elbowing shared meals off the edges of our tables. Yet, somewhere deep within us a little voice is saying, "I really should make the time to eat meals with my family," or, "I should put more care into the quality of what I'm eating," or a number of other reasonable promises. Add to this the nonstop noise—endless food choices, options for meal convenience, and the hawking of all types of "healthy" processed food—and the voice advocating the planning, preparing, and sharing of meals is lost in the din.

Here's the bottom line: the way we eat is reflective of how we value our lives. Our relationship with food is a dynamic component of how we behave, but we increasingly treat mealtime as a burden. We reduce it to an activity to be checked off the list so we can focus on our work (or something else) and continue the day. There are a host of negative associations with the daily factors of what, where, and how to eat. In *The End of Food*, Paul Roberts describes our troubled relationship with food. He says, "The very act of eating, the basis of many of our social, family, and spiritual traditions . . . has for many devolved into an exercise in irritation, confusion, and guilt."

Most Americans sincerely want to share meals with others. Purdue University's Center for Families reported that about 80 percent of families believe sharing meals is important, although only 33 percent routinely eat together. In a CASA study, nearly 70 percent of families who are not having dinner together cited the major causes are because they are too busy with work, or there are too many different activities going on that are keeping them apart. Happily, a whopping 65 percent of teens and 75 percent of parents say they would be open to cutting out an activity if it created the space for a shared meal with their family. This is an uplifting statistic begging the question: why aren't more of us doing this?

On the surface, the solution does appear simple. In families, parental leadership would be the key to getting the ball rolling. Parents who work could explore options in the workplace to create boundaries (I cover work-life balance in a later chapter), and other family members could reevaluate how many activities they are doing and reduce one or two to make room for a daily shared meal.

Yet, when I asked the question of family members, friends, and acquaintances, many felt there were a variety of obstacles keeping them from sharing meals. Some said they've avoided family dinners because everyone in the family is so amped up by the frenetic tempo of their lives they couldn't imagine spending even ten minutes together around a dining table without tension erupting. Others wanted to share meals but were intimidated, fearing they "don't know how to do it right," or felt guilty because they cannot schedule the practice with any regularity—so, why try? The topic slides off their list of priorities.

Some people I talk with wish to avoid the topic of sharing meals, because discussing it reminds them of their failure to meet expectations—their own or society's. Because planning and preparing meals was traditionally considered a woman's responsibility, a gap in domestic life became apparent as women began to enter the workforce. The challenge to fulfill that role wasn't always easy to address. Even now, in many cases it's presumed that a woman is still in charge of planning and preparing meals, which contributes to an increase in working women feeling overwhelmed. (Although one study by Project EAT showed that the frequency of family meals did not vary much based on whether the mother was a working woman.)

Single parents I talked with face a similar double-edged sword because of their additional burdens of meeting work and family commitments. Some sheepishly felt being divorced diminished their claim to some traditional family activities, such as sharing meals. There are different reactions to the emotional residue of divorce. I might have easily relinquished my "right" to this traditional ritual, but fortunately for Jini, John, and me, I was drawn to the opposite path. I looked for opportunities for ritual as a way to offset some domestic losses that would be inevitable.

People who live alone may regard sharing meals as a family event, similar to attending an exclusive club where they don't enjoy membership privileges. Many childless single people have more freedom without typical family responsibilities, so they schedule themselves with twelve—to fourteen-hour workdays. At the end of that already excessive schedule, cooking may be perceived as wasting their precious spare time.

Let's change this thinking! Let's acknowledge that no matter how busy we are and how disjointed our current eating habits may be, sharing meals can again become a powerful way of adding joy and meaning to our lives.

Redefining our ideas about the shared-meal ritual is the key: picture sharing meals as one strategy to achieve life simplification and not just another time-consuming demand.

The idea of simplicity has had some very strong advocates: Leonardo da Vinci said, "Simplicity is the ultimate sophistication." Innovator and pioneer of the personal computer revolution, Steve Jobs, also famously used this phrase to describe his design philosophy. Perhaps Jobs's confidence in this theory may alleviate any negative feelings you may have that suggest embracing simplicity is provincial. Why not embrace simplicity as a useful "lifestyle design" strategy?

What Keeps Us from Eating Together?

If eating quickly, mindlessly, poorly, and alone are symptoms, what is the root problem? What are we running toward that's making us willing to sacrifice eating well? We seem to have the notion that running faster and harder will allow us to catch up and claim our rest. I believe what we are really longing for is a less complicated, less demanding, less busy life. We want life to be simpler, to enjoy more connection with others, and to share more experiences.

Sharing healthy, delicious meals could be included in a lifestyle of simplicity. Unfortunately, the cultural demands of modern America won't change overnight. And no one is going to change them for us. We have to identify our roles in achieving better lives for ourselves.

We must accept the fact that simplification, one of the necessary factors for realignment of life balance, faces tremendous pressures. Obvious factors to consider include maintaining our work and financial commitments to take care of our homes and our children, finding the time and resources to nurture relationships, finding outlets for personal enjoyment, and making contributions to our world.

Let's take a deeper, realistic look at the obstacles to sharing meals, along with their causes and implications.

Remember that when we align our values to the way we actually want to live, we *can* design a simpler life for ourselves.

Work

Balancing work with home life is a popular concept, though in reality some workers have little, if any, control over their own work schedules. Many manufacturing, nursing, and retail employees are assigned evening or nighttime shifts, which may interfere with family life.

In many white-collar professions, modern work tools—cellular telephones, laptop computers, and BlackBerry smartphones—have created a trend of integrating work into home life as opposed to establishing a distinction between these two spheres. When we can perform work from home so easily, the separation of work and personal life becomes blurred or even invisible; many find they can't (and don't try to) resist the temptation. These working conditions seem acceptable for various reasons: we believe we're attending to our family's needs if we're physically present in the home, we may feel we have to work extended hours at home to stay competitive with coworkers, and we're satisfying the drive to further our careers at an accelerated pace.

The financial crisis that began in 2008 has created additional anxiety in the workforce, impelling many people to reinforce their financial profiles by either working longer hours at a single job or working multiple part-time jobs. And because few jobs are truly secure, some workers accept these conditions to increase their "valued employee" status and hopefully survive the next round of layoffs.

While the pattern is understandable, even the most basic daily attention to loved ones is sacrificed. We can't get that time back. We can only try to make better choices for our future. We must remember our family members and close friends are with us for life. Work and personal life can peacefully coexist, but only as parts of an established balance.

Former Lehman Chief Financial Officer Erin Callan offered regrets about her past choice to give complete attention to her role with Lehman. She says, "Don't do it like me." Callan says she didn't make a conscious choice to neglect her personal life and relationships; it just happened. She adds that women should not be afraid to ask management for "reasonable modifications" or "tweaks" so they can find the time to attend to their personal lives but still have a satisfying career.

How are employers supporting the balance of work and home lives? A recent National Study of Employers examined how 1,100 employers address the personal and family needs of their workers. Those companies best achieving the ideal of "making work 'work'" tended to be nonprofits, large organizations, and companies with racially diverse individuals in top leadership roles. The report was focused not only on documented policy but what employers reported as allowed practices.

The study also showed that 79 percent of the companies allowed their employees some flexibility in the times they arrived and left the office (up from 68 percent since the prior study ten years ago). In reviewing what the study called a "culture of flexibility and supportiveness," the researchers found that although 60 percent said it was "true" their organization had a culture of supporting supervisors who work with their employees to meet personal and family needs, management rewarded only 20 percent of those supervisors. Further, management provided a limited effort (an average of 21 percent) to promote the available employee assistance. The two major barriers to boosting work-life initiatives to support their employees were (not surprisingly) cost and the possible loss of productivity for the organization. These results illustrate that employers are knowledgeable about the challenges their workers face in achieving work-life balance, and on the face of it, they supply some resources and strategies to mitigate the problem—but there is not dedicated support for making sure those resources are used.

Due to demanding work schedules, working parents use what Cornell University researchers call "food choice coping strategies." The study of low—and moderate-income parents found working long and unpredictable hours made it challenging to establish a family meal routine. Instead, mothers were forced to compromise by skipping breakfast and using prepared or restaurant meals, whereas fathers ate while working, skipped a family meal, and used take-out options.

Couples and singles are equally prone to the toll work imposes on sharing meals. All acknowledge the difficulty of imagining how they can fit meal planning, cooking, and cleaning into their schedules without making life more complex than it already is. Couples whose schedules conflict, as well as singles who live alone, often focus on their individual responsibilities. Some are so exhausted by the hectic pace of work that they look forward to eating alone. Others may not value sharing a meal because they commonly multitask while eating, and conversation would disturb that routine. To some, sharing meals is a foreign or even uncomfortable concept. Many find the effort involved in sharing meals to be more trouble than it's worth.

Time Constraints

Current American attitudes favoring productivity propel workers into a vicious cycle. In a culture where workers are overloaded with work tasks, many feel like hostages of time. Many grind away at the to-dos on their calendars in machinelike mode. This type of lifestyle results in depleted, resentful, and out-of-control feelings.

In the book *Time Wars*, author Jeremy Rifkin examines America's attitude toward time. He describes the United States as "a nation of pioneers . . . imbued with the notion that we must keep on moving and never look back," always looking for the "new" versus looking within. Rifkin believes our relationships with time have shifted from the natural rhythms of life (when work was "organized" and "produced") to one guided by rigid operational efficiencies of the clock ("programmed" and "processed"). He argues that industrialization created tension with these relationships, which resulted in a culture with a "single-minded value of increased efficiency." This new mind-set led us to searching for automation in every corner of our lives, without an emphasis on the quality.

In 2013, The Benjamin, a New York City hotel, started offering a service called a "work down" call (which operates in the same way as a "wake up" call). This illustrates Erin Callan's point that without even knowing it, we devote excessive amounts of time to work. We need limits. I'm not at all suggesting we give up the benefits of an industrialized world or the goals of building our careers, but we must be aware of the effects on our relationships and quality of life. By acknowledging the risks, we enable ourselves to defend against them by practicing behaviors and activities that restore balance.

Our culture's addiction to immediacy allows us to overlook the reality that, as a civilized people, we need to care for future generations. Rifkin contrasts our attitudes toward time with the Iroquois Nation's progressive thinking, which considers generations past and those yet to come. They ask, "How does the decision we make today conform to the teachings of our grandparents and to the yearnings of our grandchildren?"

Corporations absolutely depend on future-oriented thinking; their CEOs lead every day with that mind-set.

How much time do we devote to strategically planning our personal lives? If we don't actively use our time toward our heartfelt priorities, the outcome will be devastating: our lives will not be meaningful.

The perception that we will never have enough time to answer to the world's demands has resulted in the now familiar operating mode: *multitasking,* a modern-day weapon against the evils of a packed schedule.

The effectiveness of multitasking has recently come into question, and it's not all that it's cracked up to be. When multitasking, we may do many things at once, but that does not mean we do any of them well. Scientists report the term *multitasking* is a misnomer, because the brain can only attend to one activity at a time and can't actually perform simultaneous tasks. Through what researchers call "highly practiced skills" (such as pouring a cup of coffee while talking on the phone), we appear to be performing common tasks simultaneously, but we are actually directing the order in which activities are being processed.

Studies are showing that there is a hefty price to pay for our multitasking ways. A study of one hundred students at Stanford University compared high multitaskers (who switch attention frequently) to low multitaskers (who switch attention infrequently). It found that the low multitaskers have better and more cognitive control. By contrast, high multitaskers are more easily distracted by irrelevant background information; they can't easily focus on what is pertinent to the task at hand.

People who make a habit of multitasking may lose their natural ability to maintain concentration. Imagine the deterioration of a society that simply can't pay attention anymore and essentially becomes a culture with self-imposed ADD-like behaviors.

In the past, I sometimes found myself simultaneously having a telephone conversation on a headset, typing an e-mail, mouthing silent responses to a coworker poking his head into my office with a question, and, somewhere in the mix, grabbing a bite of the apple sitting on my desk.

At home, I sometimes felt the same intense pressure to try to squeeze in all the obligations I could—to get all my "things" done. I would hold a conversation by squeezing the telephone between my shoulder and my head, sort mail with one hand while shoving clothes into the washer with the other, keep an eye on the pot roast, and carry on a piecemeal conversation with one of my kids. Once, sensing he did not have my undivided attention, my son asked, "Is it okay if I fly to the moon tonight?" I said, "Yes, of course, honey—(What?)" Kids know when you are not paying attention, even if you think you've fooled them by replying with a comforting phrase and a calm voice. It made me sad to realize my son felt neglected enough to test if I was listening. Even the most well-meaning parent can see it is sheer insanity to try to operate your home focused on "getting stuff done"—something I learned after burning the roast a couple of times or realizing I just tossed an important piece of mail. These mishaps were hardly catastrophes, but they still affected my quality of life. If I had the chance to make up the few years when I was burning myself out and not being present with my children, I'd do it in a heartbeat!

If you can relate to this feeling, consider how to handle the necessities and act on those that are most aligned with your values. Most importantly, focus your attention on the people you love and who are present with you every day.

As popular finance guru Suze Orman advises in relation to money, spend it on the things that are most important to you. Doesn't that concept apply to other resources in your life too? Spend your valuable resource of time on the people and activities you value most. Orman also says to get your priorities in order: first *people*, then *money* (financial security), and lastly, *things*. Thank goodness I learned to apply this rule before my family suffered any tragic personal consequences. I consider myself very lucky.

When I ask people who say they want to share meals why they do not, the most common reply is, "I wish I could, but I never have time . . . . I'm just too busy." Olds and Schwartz point out that in America, as much as we complain about our schedules, we are proud of being busy: "It serves as a badge of toughness, success, and importance." Cultural critic Barbara Ehrenreich labels this attitude "the cult of conspicuous busyness" and claims that our society perceives someone's worth based on their degree of busyness. Being busy bolsters feelings of self-worth; it means we are needed, in demand. We regard it as a virtue, because it represents the ideal of American productivity. We have a love-hate relationship with our perpetual state of activity. We have verbal duels with loved ones over who is definitively *more* busy. Being busy becomes a competition in which there are no winners.

Sometimes it's the children's crowded calendar that is the culprit. A 2009 study published in the *Journal of the American Dietetic Association* surveyed 1,687 young adults eighteen to twenty-five years old and found that most would like to share a meal with others, but 35 percent of the males and 42 percent of the females said they don't have time.

Parents want well-rounded children who will grow to be productive members of society. They set out to help their children experience enriching activities that will help them discover their talents. But sometimes this plan to develop our children misses the mark, and we get more than we bargained for. We run around wildly just trying to keep up. If childhood is experienced as a kaleidoscope of activities, how can we expect our children to grow up with the ability to prioritize their time in alignment with their values?

Admittedly, on rare occasion I allow my time boundaries to become temporarily weakened. I work myself up into a twister of goal-achievement and then feel frustrated because I can't move fast enough. When I get caught up in what Carl Honoré calls the "orgy of acceleration," I pause and take a few controlled deep breaths. I then take a moment to focus on what is in front of me. That night (and sometimes throughout the entire day) I remind myself to maintain a calmer attitude and thoughtfully detail, one by one, what matters *most*. I might put on a yoga or meditation tape and just slow everything down and "be." Slowing down requires an active process of looking at what is causing imbalance.

It's prudent to ask ourselves what the added value is in ramming as much as possible into each day.

Television and Technology

Since its rise in popularity in the mid-twentieth century, television has retained its place as a permanent fixture in most American homes. In my study, my family members named it as the form of technology most often turned on during meals. My brothers and sisters who live alone said they sometimes eat in front of the television, as it's "company" for them. Television programming has both vast appeal and a battery of viewing choices. Families often use their time together to watch favorite TV shows rather than interacting with one another in more active ways. Even when they do eat together many families eat around a TV screen. The practice of eating while distracted by TV can put people in a dissociative state, disengaged from the reality around them. It also can influence people to mindlessly overeat.

Watching television while eating poses risks to a child's eating habits. In some homes, TV is another member of the family, dictating how mealtime is conducted. Two hundred and eighty-seven elementary school children surveyed admitted eating dinner in front of the tube 42 percent of the time. Children who were not overweight reported eating 35 percent of their meals in front of the TV, but their overweight companions ate 50 percent of their meals there.

I'm not suggesting people give up television completely. But given the vast amount of television we consume, can't we turn off the TV for one hour a day to tune in to a meal with people we love?

Our increasing use of technology is directly related to our attitudes toward time, which is why so many devices are promoted as time-savers. Yet, we don't seem to effectively use the time we're saving to connect with one another. We widely choose to post a status on Facebook, send a tweet, and text message while mindlessly watching our favorite TV program, all while holding a portable food item in one hand. We screen out telephone calls to avoid conversations we think may last more than thirty seconds, but we eagerly answer texts no matter what activity we're engaged in, including meals.

It seems many people need to have a steady online presence and can't be away from their e-networking tools for any defined period of time. They need to be "streaming" themselves throughout the day. Are we afraid of becoming socially irrelevant if we're not constantly reminding people we exist? That's an awkward question, but worthwhile to ask of ourselves.

It's up to each of us to choose what kind of parameters we will use for keeping technology in its place.

However, it is certainly wise to realize we need tangible, real-life, interpersonal activities, such as sharing meals together, to offset the effects of abstracting technology.

Exercise: Separating the Wheat from the Chaff

What do you remember most vividly after reading the sections discussing how work, time constraints, and technology keep us from sharing meals? Which ideas stand out to you? Take a few moments to write a list or a description of whatever first comes to mind.

Now look over your list or description. Which detail stands out the most? Write the item on another page. Then write any descriptions, facts, arguments, stories, or memories linking that detail to your life. Ask yourself in the most accepting way possible what makes that detail meaningful to you. Is it something you see in your own life right now—perhaps even something painful—that you would like to change? Write your response.

Step 4

Aligning Values and Actions

I've learned that unless I translate my thoughts into actions, my great ideas and good intentions are like unlit candles.
—Michael Josephson

It may feel stark to admit our lives are determined by the choices we make each day. When we start thinking about what our everyday actions reveal about our priorities, we are bound to feel negative emotions, such as guilt and some defensiveness. But guilt and defensiveness get in the way of change, so we must set these emotions aside and look at our choices objectively.

To address this, we need to acknowledge we can always make time for the things we really want to do. If in our hearts we value connections with family and friends above all else, then we can't routinely deny the presence of those we care about in our lives. Instead, we need to actively plan time together, including sharing meals.

When we do not spend energy on those things that reflect our genuine values, we feel neither satisfied nor healthy. If we find ourselves day after day in a routine that is not working (such as working too much, spending too much time on the computer, and missing out on mealtimes together) it keeps us on a path away from our goals.

It's not always easy to change direction, but if we really want to effect lasting change, we must first set our intention with purpose and then take one step at a time toward the future we want to shape for ourselves. As writer Maria Robinson said, "Nobody can go back and start a new beginning, but anyone can start today and make a new ending."

To implement a shared-meal practice, we need to simply think about what we want our practice to look like, what resources and support we will use, and how the practice will become part of our lifestyle.

In today's impatient culture, we look for a silver bullet to cure our physical, emotional, and social ills. Want to lose ten pounds this week? Have a laser liposuction treatment on your lunch hour. Seeking spiritual enlightenment? Attend a two-hour seminar that will "instantly transform your life." Or perhaps you are just feeling lonely? Log on to Facebook and "poke" someone. Change is not a product for sale in a pop-up ad on the Internet or on a home-shopping channel.

We must identify our values and imagine uncomplicated everyday actions to reflect them. If we don't consciously claim our values, we may represent others by default, ones that may not be what we intend.

The good news is that implementing a shared-meal plan is a worthwhile tool for time-stressed people to further personal development, experience joy with those we love, and renew our sense of balance.

Priorities in Action

Feelings of dissatisfaction, stress, and anxiety are often the result of a dissonance among values, priorities, and the way we spend our time. Awareness of these conflicts naturally encourages change.

To make room in our lives for things that express our genuine values and priorities, we have to dismiss others. We can't continue investing in activities that don't reflect who we genuinely are; we simply don't have the time. We can't actually "have it all"—but we do get to choose from the menu.

Is our social or professional status more important than spending meaningful time with our kids, our spouse, or people who mean the world to us? Is spending a majority of our leisure time chin-deep in multimedia more fulfilling than a satisfying meal with a cherished friend, gabbing the night away? It's an important personal matter left to each of us to decide. But if we maintain that the decision is being made for us because of the challenges of our modern world, we're not being completely honest with ourselves.

We can only align our actions with our values and priorities when we're conscious of the choices we make. We must also be willing to see life balance as a continuing process. Psychologist David Gruder, PhD, author of *The New IQ,* defines life balance in three dimensions: personal well-being, connection with others, and contribution to community. Through both personal and professional experience, he has come to understand that learning to balance these three "core drives" leads to a richer and more fulfilling life.

Achieving substantial change in any area of our lives requires changing our worldview—what self-help guru Stephen Covey describes as a "paradigm shift." Some people are used to living their priorities and making choices congruent with their value system. Others have visions for their lives but sometimes make choices in conflict with that view. Covey writes that paradigms are "sources of our attitudes about behaviors, and ultimately our relationship with others." For instance, it might be clear that choosing to instant message with your friends while eating a microwave pizza rather than having conversation over a home-cooked meal with your husband reflects the relative value of these two activities. When we understand that concept, we may begin to regularly choose activities that support our values.

What we do defines us. What do we want to stand for? What do we want our legacies to be? What important goals do we have?

What unique contributions can we make? I believe that we want twenty-first-century society to be remembered as standing for something other than its obsession with consumerism, attachment to wealth, and addiction to technology. Rather, we can strive to be remembered for recommitting ourselves to the tradition of shared meals and integrating it into our lives in ways unique to our era.

The shift I'm encouraging is centered on a premise of spending time doing those things that bring us balance and joy. Living in alignment with our values can feel odd given many people feel pressured to focus on money and acquiring possessions. It's understandable (and important) that we pay attention to earning money in order to meet our financial obligations. But to live a meaningful life, we need to focus on activities that represent our values as well.

An example of a group that took on the challenge of living in accordance with specific values is the Simple Living Institute. The organization was founded in 2002 for the purpose of exploring a lifestyle called "voluntary simplicity." Its members focus less on material gains and more on quality of life. Some members choose to live in modest cottages and forego frills such as eating out or shopping for new clothes. The Institute's mission is to inspire people to break the habit of mindlessly accumulating—"find the satisfaction of enough"—while living in an environmentally conscious way. Such dramatic changes are not for everyone (including me), but its members are representative of how lifestyle choices can reflect values.

Work-Life Balance

For those of us who are not ready to change our lifestyles radically, there are many ways we can explore how to live in accordance with our values.

As mentioned earlier, many feel daily workplace obligations present serious obstacles in maintaining work-life balance. Although there is work to be done in terms of companies fully supporting employee workplace programs, many proactive companies are wisely taking notice and offering amenities and increased flexibility to retain talent, reduce burnout, and stem turnover.

Some added benefits employers see when they offer flexibility are that their employees have a higher level of engagement in their jobs and better mental health versus companies that don't offer flexibility. These employees are also more likely to be in excellent physical health and generally have a lower stress level.

Recruiters at Robert Half International, an executive recruiting firm, encourage their corporate clients to be proactive when it comes to employee turnover, including "holding regular town hall and department meetings, and one-on-one 'stay' interviews for employees to air grievances and give ways to improve the work environment."

Many workplaces offer attractive furnishings, some loosely resembling upscale hotels. It's no surprise then that some employers offer a "concierge" program to help handle a variety of issues, from getting access to popular entertainment or sporting events to handling domestic tasks such as locating a new child-care center for your preschooler. Other companies offer free lunches featuring local and organic food served in comfortable, upscale café settings. A popular California studio serves warm cookies and milk in the afternoon—a treat almost guaranteeing workers will feel pampered. Some work campuses include an outdoor activity area that leads to hiking trails or have woven a meditation garden into their corporate landscape. Still other organizations offer free yoga classes, after-hours movie screenings, cocktail parties, or recreation rooms equipped with table-top games, dartboards, or electronic game systems—all designed to relieve an intense workday schedule.

In many respects, today's workplace environments are emulating home and leisure environments. This makes it tempting to extend our time at the office, perhaps well in excess of a typical eight—to ten-hour workday. While these efforts toward an inviting workplace are greatly appreciated, for many workers, they do not directly address work-life balance. That is because no matter how enjoyable your workplace environment is, you still need to have a home life in order to create balance.

If it has been more than three months since you have paid meaningful attention to your personal needs, as well as your spouse, your kids, and your friends, consider meeting with your manager about your need to better balance your work and home life.

Before that meeting check to see if your company has a written policy regarding work hours. Next, write out a graduated wish list you'll refer to during your meeting. Start with the minimum requirements in your pursuit of work-life balance—for example, to leave work as scheduled at six o'clock or to enjoy paid time off without work interruptions. Leave space for input in the middle of the page. In this space, write anything that comes to mind, such as asking the company to provide healthy midafternoon snacks (fruits and vegetables, which won't spoil a dinnertime appetite) or ongoing flexibility in your schedule to accommodate personal, family, or educational activities. Include any considerations that would help you to stay committed to your employer, such as providing an after-school teen center or earning a one-month paid sabbatical after ten years of service. Some companies offer nutritious partially cooked or fully cooked meals—such as a tray containing lasagna, a vegetable, and salad—for employees to purchase at reduced costs. This amenity helps employees have meals with their families and increases loyalty to the employer. How about a policy of a paid day off for your birthday or a free consultation with a nutritionist? Remember, this is a wish list . . . be creative!

Finally, when making requests, keep in mind that your wishes must be grounded in reality. Your employer will not consider requests that interfere with business operations or your ability to do your job with the excellence for which you are paid.

Some corporations might be more agreeable to an open dialogue than others. Consider what might be realistic for your particular company based on its size and resources and make your suggestions accordingly. If your employer is open to considering any of your requests, it's reasonable to think they will expect you to be committed to the company as well.

The idea of approaching a supervisor about work-life balance may seem intimidating. But if you don't do it, who will? Workplace demands might continue to infringe upon your personal life unless you directly address them.

At a minimum, research the work-life balance options your company offers and identify the ones of personal value and those you can start taking advantage of today.

If you are an executive who can be an advocate for your employees' work-life balance, help shape progressive policies that best address a variety of work-life concerns. Reward your supervisors who support these policies and encourage your employees to use what your company offers.

Let's touch upon the ways we can start making changes for the better today. Create a boundary for the end of the workday—and stick to it. Promise yourself you'll resist the temptation to "finish just one more thing" before you leave. Realize there will be necessary exceptions, but have a plan. Program a reminder to sound fifteen minutes before you plan to leave and begin wrapping up promptly. To stay committed, ask those waiting for you at home to start preparing the evening meal at a certain time or establish a time and place for standing restaurant reservations with a friend.

If you must check your work e-mail after hours for urgent matters, do so only after you have enjoyed a relaxing meal with your girlfriend or taken part in another activity that is a priority to you. Only handle e-mails that truly need an answer right away.

Even though we can voice our concerns, we can't hold our employers responsible for achieving our work-life balance. This is a personal obligation for each of us.

Establishing boundaries between work and home helps us better protect our personal time. The goal should be to keep work in its place, balanced with other aspects of everyday life. Boundaries help us maintain a perspective where we can feel genuine satisfaction that we are taking care of ourselves. Ask yourself the last time you felt regret that you made time to attend your niece's graduation party or enjoyed a breakfast on your patio with your fiancé before you both left for work. You owe it to yourself to identify which work matters need your attention and which can wait.

I'm not suggesting you take such bold risks that you put your job in jeopardy. I'm simply suggesting that you need to be your own advocate and *speak up* for what is important to you, including those times when setting limits is necessary. It's certainly possible to have a win-win solution if it starts with a mutually respectful conversation.

Slowing Time

In the book *In Praise of Slowness*, Carl Honoré discusses what can happen when we slow the pace of our lives. He says when we drop our obsession with the clock, time becomes a "benign element," and loses its power to control us. According to Honoré, the stresses of modern society are giving momentum to the Slow Movement, the philosophy of which is centered on the search for true balance. Experience teaches us that doing things too quickly distracts us from our goals and mars our sense of purpose. There are certain activities that, by their design, are intended to be performed at a slower pace. Consider how you carefully examine the detail of a Degas sculpture in a museum or slowly sip a glass of wine while enjoying a sunset at the beach. Honoré recommends: "Be fast when it makes sense to be fast, and be slow when slowness is called for. Seek to live at what musicians call the *tempo giusto*—the right speed."

As mentioned earlier, in taking on too many tasks, we trap ourselves into doing them poorly. Instead, we should select a few high-equity activities and enjoy them according to their natural rhythm. Balance your checkbook efficiently, but then take your time making homemade pasta with your best friend for a dinner you'll share tonight.

As Honoré suggests, the Slow Movement touches all areas of life. When people reap the benefits of slowing down in one area, they naturally look for other areas in their lives that may also benefit by adopting a slower pace. For example, you might decide it would be more enjoyable to take a year, rather than three months, to learn a foreign language.

Slowing down your lifestyle requires reducing the number of activities you participate in or adjusting the time you'll spend on each. But how do you select the activities you'll keep on the front burner? Determine which ones bring you the most joy and further your personal goals. If a child's passion is basketball, maybe he can reconsider the karate class and soccer club. Time is a valuable commodity, so spend it doing what fulfills you, touches your soul, and reflects who you are.

The idea of prioritizing activities was played out on an episode of *The Oprah Winfrey Show*. Organizational expert Peter Walsh invited the Rathi family to participate in his Family First Challenge. The challenge was a seven-day experiment asking the Rathis to cancel all activities outside of work and school in order to reconnect as a family. During the experiment, Tanuja Rathi, freed from her responsibility of chauffeuring her three daughters to and from nearly forty hours of activities—including cheerleading, piano lessons, and tennis—found she had ample time to prepare some of the family's favorite meals. The Rathis actually ate together as a family in their home's formal dining room for the first time. Tanuja was unsure why they had never eaten there before, adding that her daughters "were so excited for this little thing!" The Rathi family rediscovered their important connection and planned to have weekday and Sunday dinners together. To make time for these dinners and other family events, each child eliminated one weekly activity—a small sacrifice compared to what they gained.

Sometimes slowing down is simply avoiding taking on something new. I'm not suggesting you ignore your desire to participate in a new activity; I'm simply saying you can benefit by making choices that factor in what you are already committed to. You can put potential new activities on a list of things you will do once you have achieved a healthy balance with your current commitments. You make the rules. Just don't get trapped in the thinking that you can do it all.

Asking family members to reduce their activities might be met with resistance. Often the best method is to lead by example. When your friends and loved ones see how much you enjoy your newly balanced life, they will wonder how you do it and be tempted to follow your lead.

Exercise: The Apple of Your Eye

Exercise A

What is your first priority in life? What tops your to-do list most often? Is taking care of your family most important to you? Connecting with those you love? Earning a good salary? Reading every day? Listening to new music?

What are some of your other priorities? Is it necessary for you to have free time to think and reflect? Is it important for you to be fit and healthy?

Starting each phrase with an action verb (earning, connecting, exercising), make a list of what is most important to you. Then number these items in the order of their importance.

Exercise B

Now imagine yourself as an objective observer. Watching what you do each day, how would that observer describe your priorities? Would she say work is the most important thing in your life? Would she note you take little or no time to take care of yourself? To that outside observer, what do your actions say about what is most important to you? What values are obvious in the way you live day to day? Make a list or write a description of your priorities and values from this new perspective. Allow yourself to feel whatever emotions arise.

Exercise C

Compare the first list of priorities with the second list made from an outside perspective. Are any of your true priorities from your first list in conflict with the priorities reflected in your daily actions? If you experience strong feelings when comparing your lists, try to accept them and remember that you're not alone. Few of us can live our true priorities constantly. But awareness of your priorities gives you the impetus to start living in alignment as much as possible.

Exercise: Easy as Pie

Change does not take effect instantly, so take one step at a time. Read through the actions in the categories below. Make a list of those actions that appeal to you, or create your own. Now look over your list. Which actions can you take right now or in the near future? Choose one that holds a lot of appeal for you and that you can start implementing today. Write the names of at least two people you can count on to support you. Explain what you're doing and ask them to check with you periodically to see your progress.

Work-Life Balance

I can check to see if my company has a written policy about work hours.

I can write a wish list that starts with my minimum requirement for work-life balance and ends with details describing my dream job. Just keep writing, no matter how small or unrealistic the details might seem.

I can find out if any flexible work options exist at my company.

I can create a boundary at the end of my workday and stick to it by making plans with others for sharing a meal at home together or meeting with friends at a certain time and location.

Slowing Time

I can take time to rationally consider how I spend my time, including thinking about which activities either harmonize or conflict with my values and goals.

I can consider one situation as it occurs and decide then whether it makes sense for me to act quickly or slowly.

Either alone or with my family, I can implement an activity plan modeled after Peter Walsh's experience with the Rathi family (the Family First Challenge) to discover which activities I can stop with few regrets and which I want to keep doing.

Step 5

Avoiding Pitfalls

The foolish man seeks happiness in the distance; the wise grows it under his feet.
—James Oppenheim

To establish shared meals as a regular practice, you must understand and expect that there will be pitfalls unique to your personal situation. The good news is that by identifying the various hidden dangers, you'll be prepared to address them.

You Need This!

If you meet resistance from friends or family members as you move toward sharing meals regularly, try mentioning theorist Abraham Maslow, who identified a well-known hierarchy of five basic human needs:

- physical needs, such as oxygen, food, water, and shelter
- safety and security
- love, acceptance, and a feeling of belonging
- esteem—both self-esteem and respect from others
- self-actualization, which is the need to find and fulfill one's potential, to be the best that one can be

Sharing meals addresses all of these basic needs by providing physical nourishment through the food shared; giving all those who gather feelings of love and security and a sense of belonging; building self-esteem through taking care of yourself and receiving respect from others that you have honored your commitment; and helping to explore your own strengths and potential in a safe and loving environment.

Getting Others on Board

Once you've decided to make shared meals a regular part of your life, be prepared to explain, persuade, and cajole your friends and family members—leading them to the same decision.

Some will react as though they've been waiting for the invitation; others will be ambivalent. Some might say sharing meals is passé or might accuse you of having lost your marbles because you know they don't have time. Perhaps they'll think you are acting strangely because you're investing time to plan something as ordinary as eating.

If you're single, encouraging others could mean telephoning friends, relatives, or neighbors, including other singles, couples, or families. Reach out to anyone you think you can persuade to want to share the pleasures and commitment of regularly eating meals with you.

As the first meal is winding down, you might propose the next time you'll get together. How about next Sunday for brunch? Or lunch on Saturday after a late-morning run?

If you're part of a couple, your partner or spouse might think it's a low priority compared to other things needing attention and suggest you revisit the topic later. Simply explain that you've read about sharing meals, you think it's important to give it a try, and you'd like your partner's support.

If you're not in the habit of eating together, surprise your partner with a favorite meal and bring up the subject of eating together more often. Visit a restaurant you went to on a first date to rekindle the warm feelings you have for each other. Explore memories of meals you each had as kids and some of the unique things your families did in celebration of meals, including holiday meals. Talk about a new meal ritual you'd like to create together that's reserved just for the two of you.

For families, introducing the subject of shared meals becomes a little more complex because of the number of people and their respective tastes, interests, and schedules. It would be surprising if all of the children in a family were to instantly agree that sharing meals is a good idea. Young children are likely to cooperate, especially if you introduce it in a matter-of-fact manner, as you do other parts of their routine (such as getting to school on time). Expect resistance from older children, remembering they may be used to following their own schedules and may only participate in family activities infrequently as it is. Some teens might say, "No way, I've got too much stuff to do . . . . Besides, I like to eat in my room while I'm ooVooing with my friends." The key in households with kids is presenting a unified vision. Round up the adults *first* to talk about and understand the plan and then approach the kids.

One incentive for moving individuals from resistant to willing is a promise they can help create the menu. Not everyone will like every kind of food, so be sure everyone's favorite foods are in rotation. It's a good idea to include at least one food item on the menu at every meal that each member of the household likes. An idea that worked with my own children was finding recipes for the dishes they enjoyed at a favorite restaurant or meals they liked while dining at a friend's house.

I included my daughter Jini in all aspects of the ritual, including selecting recipes and shopping. I remember the first time she recommended a recipe to me. She was sixteen and had just prepared a ham with an orange glaze, scalloped potatoes, and green beans for a meal at her father's house. It came out beautifully. She felt the recipe directions and photos were just the amount of detail she needed. Cooking for the family strengthened her commitment to our meal ritual.

Practically speaking, children will need time, consideration, and an open line of communication as they adjust to the new ritual. Young children may need explanations why they can no longer snack at will (so they'll have an appetite at mealtime) or why you want them to select one way in which they will help carry out the meal (because you all need to work together to be successful). Incentivize kids of any age by involving them. Offer them the privilege of being first to share the best thing about their day. You can build in other privileges for cooperative behavior, such as placing that child beside the guest of honor at the table.

The best incentives are those with apparent and logical connections to the meal. Children should be rewarded only when they have met the expectations previously communicated to them. Offering a reward as an incentive for good behavior and then delivering it regardless of how the child behaves sets up a bad precedent and reveals inconsistency. The good news is once sharing meals has been established as a routine, your ritual will relax, and most children will not only participate willingly but look forward to mealtimes.

Another strategy is to expand your audience. When my children were teenagers, I encouraged them to invite their friends over for dinner once a week. They'd enjoy making tacos before watching a video of their recent high school play. Or we'd all go to the park for a game of basketball and work up an appetite. I kept in mind particular foods (such as popcorn) that most teenagers like and included them in the meal. I asked two of my daughter's friends to take charge of the popping in an old-fashioned popper, and then we used it to garnish tomato soup. Another time, knowing Jini and her friends were discovering Indian food, I made a vegetable curry and heated some *naan* (Indian flatbread). They were surprised *naan* could be purchased outside of a restaurant.

Ultimately, some loved ones will participate wholeheartedly, some reluctantly, and some might never come around. Above all, remember the benefits of sharing meals outweigh any initial bumps in the road you might face while implementing them.

"I Don't Want to Commit"

Some adults are reluctant to commit to a regular time, because they simply enjoy the feeling of spontaneity. With good intention, they say, "Let's get together soon!" I've learned from experience (on the giving and receiving end) that "soon" is an elusive term. If you really want to share a meal with someone, it's best to be specific. Sometimes a person can't commit to a certain date on the spot, so take the initiative and phone or e-mail her to find out what works for her schedule. Be flexible but then pinpoint a time that works for both of you. In the spirit of allowing your friend freedom, let her pick the location of your meal.

In my family study, a message from the youngest generation born in the nineties came through loud and clear: they value sharing meals,

but they are reluctant to commit to a regular time because they want to maintain a fluid schedule. It's hard to change the habits of a generation that is used to autonomy from a very early age. In addition, they have endless social and other choices that compete with sharing meals. Tweens and teens may not readily accept adult guidance; parents insisting on daily shared meals might be accused of robbing their kids of their independence. But the truth is that children of all ages crave structure. Offering a family meal ritual can provide the order they need. Proceeding carefully, you might institute a ritual with lots of wiggle room that allows even the most independent children plenty of space.

"I Prefer to Eat Alone"

Some people have an innate preference for eating alone. My son told me he read that the philosopher Schopenhauer argued against sharing meals. Schopenhauer called it "vulgar," saying the physical act of eating is a private activity and can only be thoroughly enjoyed alone.

Although I am a strong promoter of sharing meals, I sometimes enjoy eating alone too. As part of my shared-meal plan, introspection and pleasure that result from a meal eaten privately are integral parts of a balanced life, as are the social connection and sense of intimacy you get from sharing meals.

You may find someone you know won't take to the idea of sharing a meal at all, as it's too much of a change for him. Don't be discouraged—continue to respectfully look for opportunities. Offer suggestions that are convenient and don't require too many changes to his routine. Perhaps he has a standard repertoire of meals he enjoys. You could prepare one of these meals and bring it to his home. You might win this person over with your considerate, gentle approach.

Your Own Worst Enemy

Your own insecurities and lack of skill can also create obstacles—ones you can easily avoid if you prepare for them and address them head on.

Consider how you might be articulating the shared meals concept with your family or friends. Sometimes at the beginning of trying something new, we have cold feet. Even though you may be committed to implementing a practice of shared meals, you may not sound sure footed. You may have concerns about the challenges that you will encounter and that might deter you from sounding confident. Keep a few core ideas in your head about what you want. For example, you might simply start by talking about what you've read and why sharing meals is important to you. Try to remember to put aside any worries and simply start with the first step. The most direct step is inviting someone to share a meal with you. Let a positive experience help you get to the second step—for example, setting a date for the next meal together.

"Planning Meals Is a Hassle"

If you want to begin or restore a routine practice of sharing meals with others, you will need some kind of plan. How else can you make the practice fit your personal circumstances? You might be put off by the word *plan*, which suffers from a negative reputation. I find having a plan helps to keep me grounded and make visible progress in my goals.

Try some simple ways to shift your perspective. Become comfortable with the idea that meal planning is much easier than it might first appear. Set aside distractions and think about the foods you enjoy eating. What's your favorite dish? Do you know how to prepare it? If not, where can you find the recipe? A family member? A cookbook? On a Pinterest board? On the Internet? It doesn't take long to think of two or three dishes you'd like to eat later in the week. Start by taking inventory of the ingredients already in your pantry that you need in order to make these dishes. (See a list of Pantry Staples in Appendix D.)

Take it slowly if that helps to relieve the stress of the process, allowing yourself an hour or so to plan a week's worth of meals. The more practice you get, the easier it will become.

Planning meals reminds me of the first time I drive to a new location. I live in Los Angeles, a sprawling city. The first time I'm driving somewhere new, it seems to take a very long time. That's usually because I'm preoccupied with associating landmarks along the way. The next time I drive to the same location, it seems to take a fraction of the time to get there, and my increasing familiarity with where I'm headed is energizing. You may find the journey in your own kitchen provides the same stimulation.

Share the meals; share the planning. Friends can take turns planning the entree for one another, while others handle the vegetables, salad, and beverages. On a recent trip to Washington, DC, several friends and I rented a condo for the week. We enjoyed our turns planning and preparing a meal for our group.

Consider a potluck for a group of friends. Send out an e-mail to those in your network, offering to host the potluck in your home. Offer that you'll make a certain dish and ask others to reply back with what they'll bring. (Evites are very helpful for this type of event.)

Couples can offer to cook for each other on alternating nights. You might e-mail a recipe to your husband and ask him to shop for the ingredients for that dish, letting him know you'll cook that meal.

If you live with a partner or family members, jump-start the planning by posting a blank piece of paper on your refrigerator and encourage other members of your household to offer their ideas and opinions about what to put on the menu. Or, perhaps you want to follow the recommendation of popular TV show host Dr. Mehmet Oz, who famously suggests, "Make it easy to do the right thing." Why not decide on four or five meals you know your family and friends will love and repeat these meals until you feel ready to add variety? There's no need whatsoever to have a large repertoire of meals in order to enjoy a shared-meal practice. Some people enjoy novelty, and others prefer the recurrence of family favorites. These are choices that are yours to make.

"I Don't Know How to Cook"

Cooking is, without a doubt, one of the most important things a person can learn. Once someone has that knowledge, that's it—they're set for life.
—Jamie Oliver

Although I'm passionate about the subject of food and sharing meals, I'm not naturally skilled in a kitchen. During certain times in my life, I have been satisfied to let others cook or relied on restaurant service, but that's changed for me over the years. I took an art class a few years ago that helped me to better appreciate the everyday beauty in my surroundings. I apply that concept to the kitchen, and I find that I truly enjoy cooking at home now. It would be easy to only sit and watch the many interesting shows that demonstrate how to cook and not do much actual cooking. Author Michael Pollan calls watching these shows a "spectator sport." When we do that, we are allowing ourselves to stay stuck! Gather some interesting ideas you can use, but then move on to creating something delicious with your own hands. These shows are appealing, because they make it look easy and the dishes are often presented in a spectacular fashion. But we have to keep in mind that there are teams of people preparing the food at every stage to make them camera ready, and what is shown to the viewer as the end result has been highly produced. See it for what it is—a television production.

In prior years, I was antsy about how efficiently I was increasing my skills in the kitchen. I decided to let that go. I am satisfied to pick up a tip here and there, and I know it's not likely I'll ever be an excellent cook—and maybe not even a truly good one. However, with the basic skills I've learned, I'm always ready to give a new recipe a shot. That's all any of us needs to start cooking for others—an open, positive attitude.

Healthy eating advocate Mark Bittman said in a recent *New York Times Opinionator* blog, "Too often we let the perfect be the enemy of the good." Get in the kitchen and have fun! Let's embrace the idea of *imperfection*! It's much more exciting and far more relaxing than living in a fantasy world where we expect everything to turn out without a flaw. Unrealistic expectations take the soul out of the experience. You may never cook like one of the contestants on *Top Chef,* so just roll up your sleeves and begin to have fun. Resist competing with or judging yourself; it only wastes time and won't help you grow confidence in the kitchen. If your cooking skills are at the level of grilling a cheese sandwich and opening a can of tomato soup, start there. Embrace that ability; offer no apologies.

Over time, if you choose, you could break a routine by varying the choice of bread or cheese or experimenting with roasted peppers or pear slices (tasty with *gruyere*). You'll expand your recipe box naturally if you're willing to take a chance now and again. I recently tried whole grain pasta with fingerling potatoes, kale pesto, and pistachios. Even though combining the pasta and potato seemed like it would not be a good idea, I decided to stick with a friend's recommendation. The combination actually worked very well. Always use the healthiest ingredients possible, and you'll present a delicious, satisfying meal.

Knowing in advance you will want to take things slowly is a good strategy to keep in mind. I have a wooden plaque on my kitchen wall that contains a Ralph Waldo Emerson quote. It advises: "Adopt the pace of nature: Her secret is patience." I frequently glance at this message and remind myself not to let a recipe overwhelm me and just take the process one step at a time. This message also reminds me to keep my hands off a dish with directions to let it simmer gently for hours.

Sometimes I borrow a phrase used by film director Ron Howard. In preparing his actors for their scene, he asks them to consider, "What's my inspiration?" Cooking is art, so taking advantage of what inspires you could be a useful method for you. For visual appeal, I ask myself, "How can I create color on a plate?" It's easy to find brightly colored food choices. I might imagine a chicken breast sprinkled with parsley and draped with roasted red pepper sauce and side dishes of asparagus and golden sweet potatoes. Whole foods have their own unique beauty. My vision is to put the color I intend for my life onto the plate.

For some dishes I emphasize taste. Recently I made a vegetarian sandwich consisting of a large portabella mushroom atop fresh sourdough bread, a drizzle of balsamic vinegar, melted smoked *gouda,* and a few sliced strawberries. The flavor combination was outstanding.

There are many different sounds that arise while cooking. Many are rhythmic and musical. When preparing hamburgers with bleu cheese and grilled onions, I love to hear the onions sizzling as they sauté and caramelize. After cooking the hamburgers almost completely, I spoon a little water into the pan and cover to steam them, which creates a rolling, percussive sound. I imagine the moisture and flavor being captured under the lid.

Your sense of touch can be an inspiration too. I always love making my mother's Italian meatballs. There's nothing like using your bare hands to mix together the ground meats, eggs, seasonings, and herbs—literally digging into the recipe. My kids used to enjoy the different feel of vegetables and various cheeses they would sprinkle on top of a pizza.

Using flavorful spices and sauces offers your sense of smell inspiration for new ideas. I recently discovered an authentic recipe for a vegetarian Thai soup called *Tom Kah Gai*, and the lemongrass and coconut made my kitchen sing. This recipe prompted me to find other Thai recipes.

Seek inspiration from *all* your senses, making the most of your time in the kitchen. Soon enough you will become skilled at building recipes based on what inspires you.

As a young mother, I found ways to add variety by choosing a different category of entrée each night. On Monday night, pizza was the main attraction; on other nights, a salad-based entrée, pasta, sandwiches, soup or a hearty stew, a vegetarian casserole, or a slow-cooked roast. (See Appendix E of this book for a Build-a-Meal Template.)

Every few months, I re-create one of my mother's masterpieces, such as her family-famous lasagna or her "chicken pieces" patties— chunks of chicken breasts added to a flour, egg, fresh herb, and *Parmigiano-Reggiano* batter and spooned into a frying pan (fried like potato pancakes). I update recipes to make them more nutritious, such as substituting spinach or whole-grain noodles in lasagna or baking instead of frying. Despite those changes, the dishes still retain the nostalgia.

Most people who've cooked with me know I'm reckless with measuring ingredients. My habit is to throw in a little of this and a bit of that. My mind-set is also stubbornly stuck on the theory that if a little of something is good, more must be better. I'm working on controlling this! For some ingredients, it might be harmless, but with others the theory doesn't stand up. I once watched a dinner guest dive across the table for a giant gulp of water after a seriously sticky, overly cheesy forkful of pasta carbonara. It was no great tragedy—and it provided a hearty laugh for everyone.

In *Relaxed Cooking with Curtis Stone*, a delicious cheese-fondue recipe is accompanied by the charming rule, "If you drop something in the pot it's a kiss for the person next to you." I appreciate Chef Stone's advice of how to promote relaxation in the kitchen: "Get your hands on quality ingredients and treat them simply."

One of the best books I've seen for beginning cooks is Jamie Oliver's *Jamie's Food Revolution*. This book is filled with pictures illustrating the various stages of preparation. Seeing the evolution gives me more confidence as I move through each step of a recipe. Oliver asks people to host a party in their homes where they commit to learning a recipe from each chapter of his book and then teach it to at least two people. What a fun way to build cooking skills in your community.

Over the years, watching the Food Network and the Cooking Channel has helped me by offering innovative ideas for side dishes— such as Giada De Laurentiis's *polenta torta*. I also picked up a very simple tip for poaching an egg on *Five Ingredient Fix*. Chef Claire Robinson recommends adding a spoonful of water around an egg cooking in a fry pan at low temperature and then covering it with a lid. The egg poaches perfectly without sticking. Thanks to cooking shows, I have also learned how to deglaze a pan to create a base for a sauce and how to quickly whip up a meringue topping. I've learned which staples I need to keep in my pantry—such as a carton of vegetable broth to add instant flavor (and less fat than oil or butter) when cooking vegetables.

Chef Alex Guarnaschelli has a charming way of describing food preparation. On an episode of *Alex's Day Off*, she added warmed cream to eggs—a process called tempering. She playfully offered, "We'll do it gradually. I associate this with the first time I introduced my parents to my in-laws. I did it in little stages, gently coaxing, gradually mixing the two elements together." In another episode, she describes how to infuse garlic into an escarole dish by stirring in a clove of garlic (held on a fork in oil for a few seconds) just prior to adding the escarole. Chef Guarnaschelli says the result is as if "somebody fabulous has just left the room and you can still smell her perfume." Recalling these types of amusing analogies will help you remain relaxed and enjoy your time in the kitchen.

Today, there are an infinite number of recipe websites available to you. The Food Network's website has many useful features: an electronic recipe box, menu plans for special events, ideas and tips for planning a party, and a search tool for locating recipes that use specific ingredients. The search tool has helped me find recipes for vegetables like sautéed radishes and fennel, which I rarely used before visiting the site. You can view online cooking videos demonstrating a wide variety of techniques.

One of the best ways to improve your skills is cooking with someone else. Grow your skills by observing and assisting someone who has more experience than you. You might find yourself asking, "Why did you sauté the onions separately from the mushrooms?" Take mental or handwritten notes. While the experience is still fresh in your mind, prepare the same dish again on your own. Then pay it forward and teach someone else, reinforcing your knowledge.

My friend Angela, who honors food and meal sharing as I do, joins me once a month to cook. We often use recipes from our respective families. Each time we meet, one of us does most of the cooking, and the other one assists, mostly watching and learning. Recently, Angela made a delicious *osso bucco*. We took pictures when it was plated, and for a few moments, we hesitated to disturb the beauty by eating it. Of course, our appetites happily took over, and we enjoyed every bite.

You can enhance your confidence in the kitchen by taking a cooking class in an area of cooking new to you. Many grocery stores, food co-ops, kitchen supply stores, and community colleges offer reasonably priced cooking classes. With each new teacher, you're bound to learn at least one new thing. I recently located a cooking class for vegetarian meals. If you choose cooking classes, don't waste a moment thinking about your skills compared to others. Everyone has strengths and weaknesses. In the beginning, focus on discovering a new flavor or learning a new technique.

Own your personal talents, and as a good friend once told me about any shortcomings you might recognize in yourself: "It's okay to look at them but just don't *stare*."

Just before the winter holidays, I invite friends to a cookie swap. Everyone brings a plate of cookies and enough copies of their recipe to share. I give each guest an empty holiday-themed plate, and everyone leaves with an assortment of cookies and recipe copies. This idea doesn't have to be limited to cookies or dessert. You can host a swap that features appetizers, beverages, entrées, or side dishes.

As an executive coach who travels extensively, my friend Jane has dined at many fine restaurants across the globe. I've talked with her at length about the spiritual power of sharing meals. I sometimes have served her dishes I've made for the first time. Even when I might feel the food I prepared is not spectacular (by professional chef standards), she is gloriously gracious. By the end of the meal, she's convinced me I've prepared the best meal she has ever eaten. She has provided a safe zone where I feel comfortable exploring new recipes. Find someone in your life who can provide a safe zone for you.

Jini's boyfriend (who calls my home Carol's Café) joins us frequently for dinner when they are in town. No matter what I'm serving, he'll take a few bites and say with humor and appreciation, "I'd take a punch in the face for this." It's a quirky statement I never tire of hearing. It inspires me to keep trying new recipes.

Learning to be a better chef can be an exciting lifelong goal. You may never completely master the art of cooking. With so many kitchen adventures awaiting you, why would you want to?

The key is to have an abundance of patience with yourself and don't try to be perfect. Just have fun. Soon, you will confidently say that you *can* cook.

"I'm too Tired to Cook"

Fatigue is another of the leading reasons why people don't cook and share meals with others. At the end of the workday, even thinking about preparing a meal can seem daunting. My own active job often leaves me tired at the end the workday. I could decide that I'm too tired to make dinner, but then I would regret missing the experience of cooking and sharing a meal. For me, it's a daily activity I treasure, and my life is better for it. So, when I'm feeling tired, my technique is really quite fundamental. I simply walk into the kitchen and begin the process of preparing food. I open the windows for fresh air and light, turn on additional lights if needed to invite more energy, and turn up the music. Singing along with classic Broadway show tunes while chopping vegetables is a ritual I have too. Use whatever you have at your disposal to cultivate an ambience that inspires you to create.

I find a proven way to generate aroma in the kitchen is to sauté a fresh tomato in a splash of olive oil; I always have a tomato handy just for the purpose of putting me in the cooking mood. I have a basil plant on my patio just off the kitchen, and I'll tear off a few leaves and chop them up. The aroma of the freshly chopped herb and tomato convinces me there is no place more reenergizing than the kitchen after a long day.

You may find that creating and then enjoying a meal in good company sets a tone of pleasure well into the rest of your day or evening.

Exercise: The Carrot and the Stick

Think about your objections to establishing a regular shared-meal practice. At the top of a sheet of paper, write these column headings: "Resistance from Others" and "Resistance from Me." In each column, list as many types of resistance as you can that prevent you from sharing meals.

Now look at the two lists. Which list feels heavier to you right now? The list that has more items might not weigh as heavily on you as the shorter list, so choose according to your feelings. Then, based on which list feels heavier to you, choose one of the exercises below and complete one of the challenges for that exercise.

Exercise A: Resistance from Others

If early resistance from your partner, spouse, friends, or family members weighs heavily on you, choose a challenge from the following list that you can begin to implement today. Whichever challenge you choose, remember that respecting and cooperating with each other is the best way to reach your goal.

Challenge 1: Have a Heart-to-Heart

Choose someone you trust for a heart-to-heart. Explain your desire to routinely share meals with people you care about. If she is someone who wants to share meals but has qualms, try to determine what those concerns are. Ask, "How can I help to make meals together a priority for you?"

When you discover the cause for reluctance, try to work out a plan for sharing meals that will work for everyone. If your potential dining partner doesn't like to cook, ask if she would do the shopping, invite other guests, set the table, light the candles, or wash the dishes. Many tasks besides cooking go into making a shared meal, and your friend is likely to be good at (and willing to do) at least one of them.

Challenge 2: Cook with Someone Else

Invite someone to cook with you. If that person declines, ask another until someone says yes. Plan a meal featuring one dish you've cooked before and one dish the other person has cooked before. Prepare the dishes and eat them together. Afterward, talk about your experience. Discover what you've learned from each other about the ingredients or cooking methods.

Challenge 3: Wooing through Food

If you're already a good cook, use your cooking skills to persuade reluctant friends and family to dine with you. Once your companion has been satisfied with good food, make a case for sharing meals on a regular basis. If you accept this challenge, don't hesitate to let your fellow diners know you won't do all of the cooking every time (explaining you don't want to deny them the pleasure of cooking). Instead, you can decide how to share the responsibilities for the meals, each person contributing in line with his talents, which will invariably grow.

Challenge 4: Create Your Own Challenge

If none of these challenges feels quite right, create a challenge of your own that you can start today. Think about whom you'd like to share meals with. Think about personalities and any reluctance they might feel about sharing meals. Think about why they are reluctant. How can you respectfully address those issues? Can you persuade them to try sharing meals with you once a week, perhaps in exchange for some new activity they would like you to try? Explore the meal that would be the easiest one for this person to share. Perhaps breakfast is your wife's favorite meal and, therefore, an option to consider.

Exercise B: Resistance from Me

If your own resistance weighs heaviest on you, choose a challenge from the following list that you can begin to implement today. Remember the only way to reach your goal of sharing meals with others is a calm, thoughtful breakthrough. If it's something that you really want to do, keep thinking about ways you can address your feelings and don't give up.

Challenge 1: Time Out

For one week, set aside ten minutes a day to simply sit and think. If you have a family and ten minutes of alone time is difficult to find, consider sitting quietly in your car, escaping into the bathroom, or claiming a quiet corner of the backyard. Think about whatever you like—how much you want to check your iPhone, for example—but don't do anything. Just notice how you feel physically. You might feel twitchy or impatient. Or, you might feel relaxed.

After one week, continue setting aside ten minutes a day to sit and think, but this time, consider the subject of shared meals. Think about your reasons for picking up this book. A part of you knows the fulfillment that sharing meals can bring. Allow the voice of resistance to come into your mind, and when it says something like, "Preparing meals is just one more thing I'll be expected to do," respond in an encouraging way. Consider, "I've wanted to start a meal ritual for a long time, but I can't do it all myself. I'm going to talk with my husband and see if he'll join in and help. Maybe we can start small by having dinner together once a month." Imagine in detail how one of these dinners will look.

Challenge 2: One-Dish Wonder

Sometimes just the thought of change can be paralyzing. You know what you want, but you don't know how to get there. Start exactly where you are, wherever that is. If you dream about preparing delicious and nutritious meals for friends and family but you feel uncomfortable in the kitchen, start with a modest goal. Choose one dish and practice making it until you're confident that you can call it your specialty. If you're a beginner, choose a simple dish, such as a potato casserole or a Crock-Pot of chili. Make sure it's something you like and something that's good for you—you'll most likely be eating a lot of it. Desserts have their place, but save those for later. When you think you have the hang of making your specialty dish, feed it to whoever will eat it with you. Then invite that person to bring his own specialties to dinner for you to try.

Challenge 3: Spilt Milk

What is your relationship with food? What kind of experiences have you had sharing meals with others? If negative past experiences are keeping you from sharing meals, set yourself up for success (and healing) in ways that build your confidence, create positive associations, and move you toward your goal of regularly sharing meals. Imagine a comfortable scene involving food and other people. Maybe right now that means sharing an appetizer and a drink with a group of friends in a public place where you can leave whenever you wish. Maybe you would feel comfortable talking with a coworker over a cup of coffee. Start wherever you are, keep your goal in mind, and take the next comfortable step toward it.

Challenge 4: Create Your Own Challenge

If none of these challenges feels quite right, create a challenge of your own—something you can start today. You know yourself better than anyone else, so you are in the best position to identify and address your resistance to sharing meals.

Step 6

Planning and Preparing Shared Meals

When you're dying of thirst, it's too late to think about digging a well.
—Japanese proverb

Why Planning Can Help

In a world where we are offered much freedom, a spontaneous way of life is appealing. Although spontaneity may have its place in your shared-meal plan, a degree of structure is necessary to make sharing meals part of your lifestyle. Once you are in the habit of sharing meals, you will appreciate that you took the time to make a plan ensuring you'll have more enjoyable meals together.

Planning can create excitement. When my kids were young, I posted the week's menu on the refrigerator. They said it was exciting to see what we were eating for the week and often contributed to the menu for future weeks. Planning a meal also helps you attend to specific details pertinent to that meal. When I wanted to create a Mexican-themed dinner for *Cinco de Mayo*, I shopped for a centerpiece platter in the shape of a sombrero and bright red, green, and yellow cloth napkins. For a springtime dinner, I used a sunny white and yellow tablecloth, serving a tossed salad with shredded chicken and mint leaves and adding fresh lemon slices to the table water. These ideas are so simple to create and take very little planning, little effort, and little or no additional cost. What do you want your shared meals to look like? Everything starts with your vision.

Another benefit of planning is it saves time. If you plan to eat as one group, you only need to buy ingredients for that one meal. At first, people in your home might rebel against no longer being allowed to order a customized meal as if in a food court at a mall. Trust that in time they will accept and even prefer the new simplicity. They may discover a new favorite food as a result of trying dishes other people enjoy.

When you plan meals, you also become more organized—a time-saver when you shop. Writing out a list in advance of a trip to the market can save a last-minute run—say, to pick up the blackberries you wanted to add to a fruit salad.

As you become more comfortable cooking at home, you will save even more time. For example, you learn how long it takes to parboil the kale, how many minutes it takes to soften the sautéing chopped carrots, which items you can leave on the stove to simmer, and which ones you need to watch carefully.

Sometimes we make the mistake of thinking that because we've tripped down a stair, we should just allow ourselves to continue falling down the whole stairwell. If we give in to that way of thinking, we're committing self-sabotage. For example, you might have decided your shared-meal plan will consist of five weeknight meals, but for the last three nights you haven't been able to make even one meal work, leading you to feel like you want to scrap the whole idea. It might seem tempting to give up, but I strongly encourage you to keep trying! Even if you have a rough go of it at first, it *will* get easier. Be patient with yourself and keep your eye on the goal. You've learned about all the ways in which you can create more joy and life balance through meals, so it's worth your while to keep on your plan.

Planning will also help you to feel in control of an important part of your life—the harmony of your actions and values. Even if you run into a rough patch now and again, don't give up. Stanford psychologist Albert Bandura offers that how well you believe you can perform a task or overcome an obstacle is critical to how well you will actually perform. If you can envision yourself successfully planning, shopping, and preparing delicious meals, the thought process itself will actually help you achieve your goals.

How much planning is right for you?

When beginning a shared-meal practice, some people need lots of structure. They might plan everything in detail using charts and lists. Some might hold regular family meetings to check on their plan's progress or shop for groceries on the same day each week. Others like the free flow of setting aside a half hour at the end of each day to pull out a quick recipe and shop just before preparing a meal. There is no right or wrong way. Experiment until you find the structure that feels most natural but still allows you to have a plan of some kind.

Think about the resources and strategic planning that help you achieve goals in the workplace. Do you find project plans useful?

Have you observed how those in leadership roles use the help of planning documents to implement changes for their organizations? Well, there's no reason why you can't use these same planning tools to help you advance your home organization goals, including shared meals.

If this idea appeals to you, take a look at the Shared-Meal Project Plan I've created as your guide. This *project-plan* approach may be too formal and structured for some, but for others, it will be exactly what is needed to get started.

Begin by reading through the sample plan. Ask yourself, "Which parts, if any, of this structured approach appeal to me? Which elements make sense for my lifestyle? Will this approach help me develop a shared-meal plan (or better organize my current one)?" Then, modify the sample plan (see below and Appendix C) as needed to create your own personalized plan.

This plan can work if you have a family, have a partner, or are single. Use this guide as is or customize it to your circumstances.

Project Plan Example:

Vision statement: describes the guiding image of your shared-meal plan's success.
Example: My vision is to develop opportunities for balance, joy, and meaningful connection through sharing meals with family and friends.

Mission statement: describes the specific activities that will achieve your vision.
Example: I will make sharing meals a priority by finding at least one opportunity to share a meal with someone each day.

Values: describes the characteristics that underlie the vision.
Example: We represent the values of interpersonal connection, simplicity, and balance through sharing meals with others.

Short-term objectives: describes one or more immediate goals.
Example: (a) My dining partners and I will plan the meals in advance, each of us assuming a helpful role; (b) During the meals, we will have a tech-free, distraction-free zone so we can be fully present with one another.

Long-term objectives: describes the goals that will take longer to achieve and are wider in scope than the short-term objective.
Example: (a) My family or dining partners will shop together and choose ingredients to keep our meals nutritious; (b) Once we have a ritual that feels natural and is working smoothly, we'll invite others to join us (neighbors, friends).

Action plan: describes a set of specific steps to help you achieve your objectives.
Example: (a) My dining partners will commit to the frequency of our plan (We'll share weeknight meals together, Saturday breakfast, and Sunday brunch.); (b) We'll each agree to pitch in (One person will shop, another will cook, and another will set/clear the table, etc.); and (c) We'll commit to a three-month trial period.

Strategy evaluation: describes how you will assess if your plan is on course.
Example: On Sunday of each week, we will have a check-in to discuss which parts of our plan are working and which parts are not. (Are too many activities getting in the way?)

Performance measurement: describes how you will measure the performance of those in your plan.
Example: Once a month, we will have a roundtable discussion to see if everyone is performing the activities they have agreed to do, working in the spirit of cooperation.

Corrective action: describes how you will change methods or strategies to get on course for fulfilling your goals.
Example: At our monthly meeting, we will discuss what roles will be shifted to keep everyone motivated; we'll agree upon next steps. (Do we need to revise the time we are eating together?)

Another approach to planning shared meals uses elements of a *spiritual ritual* to create a framework (see Appendix C for a template you can use). My friend Dora, a Reiki master, helped to create this alternative approach.

Dora points out that because leadership is important in any ritual, one person should act as the leader. As the ritual develops over time, others may choose to lead future gatherings.

Spiritual Ritual Example:

Grounding: As the leader of the ritual, you agree to host the first shared meal. You set the tone by offering your commitment to a calm and loving shared-meal practice.
Example: You propose the elements of the Sacred Space *you'll share, the* Tools *you'll use, your* Intention, The Heart *you will all dedicate to the meal, and the* Closing/Give Thanks. *(These elements are described below.)*

Sacred Space: You discuss locations and decide where your shared-meal ritual will take place. Before each meal, free the space of distraction in order to promote peaceful feelings and positive energy.
Example: We will share our meals in our dining room, which will be free of technology and will be decorated in colors that encourage feelings of well-being. We will light candles and play music to enhance the spirit of the meal.

Tools: Consider what physical materials you will need to create a meaningful shared-meal ritual.
Example: We will incorporate the use of healthful ingredients, seasonings, cooking utensils, and beloved recipes handed down from our relatives. In the center of the table, we will set items that symbolize the values of those gathering.

Intention: An agreement is made to set the intention to ensure the best possible shared-meal experience.

Example: Prior to each meal, the leader will announce the intention of the shared meal, emphasizing connection with one another and gaining nourishment from the food and the experience. Then, the leader will softly ring a bell to indicate the beginning of the meal.

The Heart: During the meal, we will honor those gathered around the table.
Example: Listen with an open heart so that all participants feel the security of a loving and safe environment to share conversation. Take a moment to remember those no longer with you and send them loving thoughts about meals you've shared in the past.

Closing/Give Thanks: As you conclude the shared meal, offer thanks.
Example: Each person offers thanks for everyone's role in making the meal happen. The leader concludes the shared-meal experience by softly ringing a bell.

--

Now that you've read through two different approaches to planning a shared-meal ritual, take a few minutes to list the ideas that seem useful.

My wish is that you will be able to take what you've read in one or both plans and devise a plan that feels right for *you*.

Remember that although guidelines help to make shared meals beneficial for all involved, there is no need to make your guidelines strict unless that's what you want. You can keep your plan loose, but not so loose that it lacks any shape or form. Everyone should be able to recall the plan's basic features—such as "We all gather Monday through Friday at six o'clock and Saturday and Sunday at two o'clock," or "My boyfriend does the shopping after work, and I set the table before he gets home. We cook together." The first steps of your plan should seem easy to you (almost effortless), so you can begin to see results right away.

Who's Coming to Dinner?

When you envision your ideal shared-meal practice, who is sitting at the table with you? If you're single or part of a couple without children, does the company vary? Perhaps you picture a quiet dinner with a friend or loved one. Imagine a dinner party for a larger group and who might be at the table. If you're implementing shared meals for your family, do you want to invite neighbors, extended family members, your children's friends, or other close family friends? If so, think about how often you'd like to limit your meals to your immediate family and how often you'd like to have guests. There's no right or wrong approach. If you want to invite guests only on holidays, then that's what you should do. If you change your mind about any aspect of the plan at any time, simply adjust your shared-meal plan accordingly. It's *your* plan, and there are no rules— only the guidelines and elements you create. Take ownership of what you develop, making modifications as you see fit based on those included in your plan.

Let the Games Begin!

After you have decided who you'd like to share your meals with, it's time to speak with those people. If you are single and living alone, this step may mean talking with several friends or family members to gauge how willing they are to help you reach your goal. If you live with a spouse or children, gather everyone for a family meeting. Present your ideas for a shared-meal plan based on ideas you have developed before the meeting, but encourage each family member to help shape the plan. Getting others' thoughts will help you engage them emotionally, which will only serve to help your overall efforts.

Children in your house should have some input, ideally by influencing elements that play to each child's strengths. For instance, you might say, "Christina, I really enjoy the artwork you have been creating in Mr. Walker's class. I think they might make pretty decorations in our dining room. Would you like to select a few pictures we can hang together?" Or, "Matt, would you like to help prepare a fruit salad? You told me last week you discovered mango, so I thought we might try it with other types of fruit to create a dessert."

Explain that each family member will have a role to play, and each role helps create the benefits of the shared-meal experience. Some roles (such as clearing the table and washing the dishes) might be perceived as less desirable than others. If that is the perception in your family, consider posting a chart to rotate roles from week to week. (See Appendix B for a sample Activity Chart.) Rotating also lets everyone in the group practice a variety of skills over time. Offer children age-appropriate duties, including watching adults perform more advanced tasks.

For small families, a rotation chart might be too much structure. It may be more practical to simply gather together at a certain time to start the meal activities and end with your family members cleaning up together.

The role my son played in our family meal ritual was contributing to menu ideas, shopping or carrying groceries in from the car, setting the table, and filling water glasses throughout the meal. For him, eating the food was the highlight, and John would jokingly say it was his primary role. In retrospect, I wish I had encouraged him to be more hands-on in the food preparation when he was a kid, but as an adult, he's now growing his skills. Today he is always in charge of providing the background music. He also spots any unused silverware, saving the person whose job it is to wash dishes from any unnecessary work. In our home, we call these pieces of silverware "blessings," a term used by my stepmother-in-law's mother, a vibrant ninety-five-year-old woman with the delightful name of Betty Pennypacker.

From a young age, my daughter took an active interest in what was cooking in the kitchen. She often questioned the choice of ingredients and thus became adventurous in her choices. As an adult, she continues to learn innovative ways to prepare food. When we're in a restaurant together, we discuss the process we think the chef used to prepare something delicious we're eating, and we talk about how we can duplicate the dish at home.

Some families don't need lists and rules to keep them invested. For example, if self-motivated family members know they are expected to start preparing a meal at six o'clock on Sundays, Wednesdays, and Fridays, all they might want is a menu posted on the refrigerator with names next to each dish indicating who is responsible for preparing it. Other ways you can keep your meal activities unified is to shop together one time a week or, if you have extra time, spontaneously offer to help someone else with an activity he is doing. Create a realistic, general plan to fit both your family's strengths and shortcomings. If you know from experience that your family tends to lose organization without a structured plan, create one, as it will set you up for success.

When you choose to implement a shared-meal practice, you choose to lead. If you delegate well and allow space for your companions to adjust to the practice (and some time to whine about it at first because of the changes in their routine), the benefits will buoy you. If you feel frustrated, angry, or put-upon in meal planning or preparation, this usually means some aspect of the practice conflicts with your values and priorities. Or, it might mean you have not solicited enough help from your family or friends. If so, take a moment to acknowledge what is at the core of your dissatisfaction and make adjustments. The last thing you want is to commit to a shared-meal practice and not enjoy the experience. If your children dislike your menu choices, sit down with them, acknowledge their complaints, and ask them to help you think of healthy alternatives. By taking swift action to change what's not working, you will dispel feelings of being a victim, and your dining partners will get the message you are devoted to making a shared-meal practice work.

Where Are We Eating?

When you think about sharing meals, where do you see yourselves sitting? Are you at specific seats around the kitchen table, in a formal dining room, or at the counter of a diner? Does a meal count as shared if you're eating in a restaurant? Sure it does, at least as long as interaction is part of the experience. According to the National Restaurant Association, the American restaurant industry is a $632 billion-dollar-a-year business; an astounding 48 percent of the food dollar is spent in restaurants. Clearly, eating in restaurants is a popular venue for meal sharing.

The quality of the environment where you share meals makes a huge difference in the experience, so when eating out, pay close attention to the ambience. Some restaurants have delicious food, but the environment may be very excitable. Maybe some nights that is what you are looking for, but other nights you'll go elsewhere as you want to take your time.

If you and a loved one have a favorite restaurant (such as one with a table in a quiet nook), there's no reason to stop eating there. Integrate this restaurant into your meal-sharing plan. My friend Linda and I participated in many marathons together over the past twenty years. After our weekly training routine, we stopped at a café on a golf course located at the end of our walking route for delicious eggs with salsa verde. This post-training breakfast became part of the shared-meal routine my friend and I enjoyed many times together.

Sometimes in restaurant settings you will make new friends and extend the circle of your ritual. A coworker of mine did just that. One evening, she and her husband were enjoying a cocktail in the lounge of a restaurant while waiting for their table to be ready. They made friendly conversation with a couple who mentioned they also visited the restaurant every Friday night, so they invited the couple to join them for dinner. Now they have a standing double date.

If you find yourself looking for a dining partner, seek restaurants offering family-style dining—long communal tables that promote making new friends.

If you are going to make eating out a regular activity in your shared-meal practice, bear in mind many restaurants serve foods that are less nutritious or less healthfully prepared than home-cooked food. Chain restaurants buy food in bulk, often shipped from hundreds of miles away. The dollars you spend in restaurants encourage trends. Patronize those who use ingredients from local growers, who encourage healthy eating by offering a menu that includes healthy options, or who are willing to modify dishes to suit your needs.

If you eat at one of the many restaurants that serve oversized portions, be mindful of the amount you're eating, or you might eat more than you intended. This might be because there is so much food on your plate you lose track of how much you've eaten, you don't want to waste the extra money you've spent eating out, or you don't like the idea of doggie bags. You can positively affect your dining experience at a restaurant by asking your server to put salad dressings or entrée sauces on the side or by regulating the bread basket—take a piece if you wish and then ask the server to remove the basket so the warm bread doesn't tempt you. When I am served gigantic portions, my new habit is to cut the serving in half (or smaller) and ask for a take-out container for the rest. You can find similar strategies in the book *The Get with the Program! Guide to Fast Food and Family Restaurants* by the popular author and exercise physiologist Bob Greene.

You can develop your palate by visiting restaurants that serve ethnic foods you may not ordinarily cook at home, such as Spanish *paella* (a multiflavored rice dish) or a Korean favorite, *bibimbap* (a layered rice, beef, and vegetable dish). You may not always love the new tastes, but exploring ethnic restaurants will surely give you and your fellow diners an expanded range of choices, ideas for new dishes to create at home, and some food adventures. This strategy is one my friend Olga and I use. I came to realize the benefits of discovering new dishes through a great book, Eve Zibart's *The Ethnic Food Lover's Companion*. Zibart's book has a wealth of historical information about native food cultures and distinctive dishes around the world and is a helpful guide for exploring ethnic foods.

Many who regularly share meals eat primarily at home or at the homes of friends or relatives. Eating in a private environment allows us to focus on the food and on each other without distractions, such as subliminal pressure to hurry and eat because other customers are waiting to be seated. By eating together in spaces we control, we also feel more comfortable talking about personal or private matters.

What's on the Menu?

Never eat something that is pretending to be something else.
—Michael Pollan

There's no doubt about it: food industry advertisers have captured our attention. Adults and children alike are affected by what they see, but children may be even more influenced to make poor nutrition choices. Dr. Daheia Barr-Anderson and a team of researchers at the University of Minnesota studied two thousand students in middle and high school and found a direct link between watching more than five hours of television a day and five years later exhibiting a diet full of fried and fast food, sugar, and trans fats. Barr-Anderson says television ads feature actors who seem physically fit, so adolescents may not get the message about the lack of nutrition in the products. This study unfortunately also showed that there were scarce advertisements for nutritionally sound foods to balance the unhealthy influence. According to the Kaiser Family Foundation, "Preteens absorb more than 7,600 commercials a year for candy, sugary cereal and fast food." Eighty percent of obese teenagers will continue their struggle with weight into adulthood. Many turn to diet pills or liposuction or develop an eating disorder to manage their weight. Children of all ages can develop Type II diabetes as a result of unhealthy eating and quite possibly die at a younger age than the generation that raised them.

The bottom line is we need good food to fuel our bodies and maintain good health. The best way to promote this ideal is to prepare the healthiest meals possible and to talk with each other about why what we eat matters. Choose recipes that call for whole grains, fresh produce, and little or no partially-hydrogenated oils. Avoid items containing high-fructose corn syrup. Reduce or eliminate your family's consumption of unhealthy snack foods, especially soda (which is not only a nutritionally empty food but is loaded with refined sugar and can cause serious health disorders, including obesity, diabetes, and heart disease). Here's an easy drink to make as a substitute for soda: add eight ounces of seltzer water to a small amount of fresh juice (about one-eighth cup of any juice). I've been using this formula for years, and it's such a refreshing way to kick the soda habit.

If you buy ready-made items or complete meals to supplement the ones you make yourself, look at the ingredients listed on the package. Be aware that the frequent use of the word *natural* on labels doesn't necessarily mean the contents are healthy. By FDA standards, it means no added color, flavors, or synthetic substances. Many fats, salts, and sugars occur naturally, and the food could still be processed in a way that no longer preserves what was once naturally healthy for you.

Snacks

Today, there is a glut of truly unhealthy boxed snacks on the shelves at your local supermarket. Strongly consider a policy to remove those items from your shopping list. Instead, keep high-fiber, low-fat granola bars and a variety of nuts, cheese sticks, cucumber slices (delicious sprinkled with cumin and lime), baby carrots, hummus, nonfat yogurt, and fresh fruit on hand. My kids liked frozen grapes or chilled, sliced apples sprinkled with cinnamon or dipped in yogurt. You can't prevent your kids from getting junk food from other sources, but that doesn't mean you need to abandon standards in your home.

Some families have a no-snacking or one-snack-a-day policy and feel this is one way to encourage healthy eating habits. My parents took great care in responding to our needs, but they didn't perform cartwheels whenever one of their children wanted something. There was a hierarchy of priorities, understood by everyone. Perhaps we had a slightly rumbling belly on occasion waiting for lunch or dinner to be served, but we also had appetites at mealtime. Author Paul Roberts writes that in past generations people expected to feel mild pangs of hunger between meals, which they likely considered normal. For adults and children today, sometimes a need seems to be answered by a disproportionate call to action.

There is a place for healthy snacking in a successful shared-meal plan. A practical strategy is to encourage your appetite to develop naturally by eating three meals a day and having a light snack—such as a piece of fruit, a few bites of vegetables, or a small handful of nuts—once in the morning and once in the afternoon. So you don't get overly hungry, it is a good idea not to lapse more than six hours between meals.

Shopping

Once you've decided on several meal choices, decide how far in advance you want to shop for groceries. How many meals do you want to shop for in each shopping trip? Will you be eating leftovers some nights? Will you shop on a particular day of the week? I shop midmorning every Sunday, stopping by a local fruit and vegetable stand and then a small market, purchasing everything I'll need for the next five days. I shop with a prepared list, after I've enjoyed a healthy breakfast (so I can resist impulse food buys). On Saturday, I buy food for same-day meals or eat at a restaurant that evening. If you have a large family—or if the foods you buy include lots of fresh fruit, green leafy vegetables, or other perishable items—you may have to shop more than once a week.

Regardless of whether you're cooking from recipes or memory, make a list of everything you know you will need to buy. If you prefer to be somewhat spontaneous or you're unsure what you want to cook, you can seek inspiration from what you see in the market. Make a basic shopping list but take a chance by picking up a vegetable or fruit you've never tried before and discover if you like it. Understand that if you don't shop with specifics in mind, you might need to make an extra trip or two throughout the week. Try out a few different methods and find what works best for you.

I find shopping is most enjoyable when I'm not in a hurry. If you feel this way, give yourself plenty of time so you're not forced to make hasty decisions. Search out local farmers' markets when the season is right. Produce is often fresher, less expensive, and has more flavor than produce sold in large supermarket chains. Buying locally is good for the environment and small business, and it promotes health without digging deeper into your pocket.

Dr. David L. Katz, a nationally renowned preventive health expert, compared the purchase price of popular, processed consumer items versus other items considered more nutritious. He found that in many categories (such as breads, dairy, and cereals) the healthier product is only marginally more expensive (he claims pennies). He recommends exploring bargains in store-brand versions and making meals from scratch to save money. I've been shopping for organic food for several years, and I find Katz's assertion true. Many organic and nonorganic foods are fairly comparable in price. My budget has not changed much, but I feel better because the quality of the food I eat is better. (See Appendix H for information on The Politics of Nutrition.)

Try to buy a high volume of fruits and vegetables. Think about how to incorporate them into the center of your meal and not only as a side dish or dessert. When you can, buy organic foods—especially for dairy, meat, and thin-skinned fruits and vegetables, which typically have greater effects from pesticides, hormones, and antibiotics that may have been used when the food was produced. Refer to websites that offer current data on the dirty dozen (foods typically containing higher amounts of pesticides) versus the clean fifteen (those lowest in pesticides). Get comfortable with reading labels.

Shopping with people who will be eating with you is a great way to get new ideas. It can be fun to see how individual ingredients shape up to an entire meal you've created together. Check with your dinner partners to see if anyone wants to go shopping with you.

Preparing Meals

I still think that one of the pleasantest of all emotions is to know that I, I with my brain and my hands, have nourished my beloved few, that I have concocted a stew or a story, a rarity or a plain dish, to sustain them truly against the hungers of the world.
—M. F. K. Fisher

Cooking

Once you consider the kitchen a place to experience the many aspects of food, you may actually find your time there therapeutic. Preparing a meal and becoming fully engulfed in the experience (for its own sake and aiming for improvement) often puts me in the psychological zone that psychologist Mihaly Csikszentmihalyi calls "flow," the state of mind when someone is experiencing oneness in both physical and psychic energy.

We are a society that handily provides rewards—in some instances—for little or no measurable achievement. We might take action only when there's a guarantee of a reward. We have become accustomed to being extrinsically motivated (from outside influences), and frankly, it cheapens our life experiences. When both children and adults take the step forward into the kitchen with the goal of just getting involved, they grow together and lay the foundation for long-term habits. This is because intrinsic motivation (motivation from within) carries the process of self-discovery and our personal attachment. Therefore, goals achieved through intrinsic motivation are more successful in the long run than extrinsic ones.

A Johns Hopkins study suggested that efforts in the kitchen may have unexpected benefits. Although this study was based on mice, it suggests that food people help to prepare may taste better simply because they had to do some work to get it. The study also shed some light that food prepared by others might relate to overeating. Because eating food someone else has made for you is a more abstract experience, a person may eat more of it as an attempt to compensate for the missing satisfaction of not having been involved in its creation. This information could serve as a strong motivation to get others involved in preparing food.

As I've mentioned earlier, take it slow and easy. Get plenty of assistance, if possible, and go through each recipe together, working through any problem spots one step at a time. If you're an experienced cook but are used to cooking alone, invite someone into the kitchen with you. If you're not ready to give up any cooking control, at least that person can keep you company and will learn from observing you.

Another strategy I find helpful when preparing meals is to cook an ingredient once and repurpose it for additional meals. For example, for three meals in a week, I'll buy a pound of chicken breast. I'll sauté the chicken in lemon and herbs and serve it with brown rice and asparagus for one meal. I'll use some of the leftover chicken in a soup with chicken broth, peas, carrots, and shallots for another. For the third meal, with the remaining leftovers, I will serve it cold as I create a Chinese chicken salad with peanuts and mandarin oranges. (See Appendix F of this book for Recipes, Cooking Skills, and Related Resources.)

Alcohol is an optional addition to a meal, depending on the circumstances and who is gathering. I occasionally drink a glass of wine at dinner, although I didn't when I was raising young kids (mostly because I can get tipsy on a single glass). For some families, alcohol is a normal part of the dining experience. During my childhood, wine was served at our large Sunday gatherings. I remember family discussions about how wine is made, the various types of wine, and where wine grapes are grown. We had a small backyard vineyard (growing wild and definitely not for production), so it was intriguing to connect the plant to the wine. If you're a parent who chooses not to consume alcohol at meals, you might consider finding a way to introduce the topic of alcoholic beverages to your children.

When you're ready to serve the food, put it on platters and into bowls to pass around the table. Everyone (even very young children, with a little help) can practice serving themselves appropriate portions. Even if you're sharing a meal with only one other person, it's still a good idea to pass containers of food to each other rather than serve portions directly from the stove. This approach is more personal and gives you the positive psychological benefits of sharing.

Preparing the Table

Sometimes a dining table becomes crowded with books, mail, and other odds and ends. I've been in many homes where the table is overtaken by correspondence, computers, papers, and miscellaneous items. The person who prepares the space for eating should begin by completely clearing the table. If you don't have a separate dining room, consider setting up a standing screen or curtain to make a private dining space. Doing so sends the message that mealtime is important.

After the table is cleared, you can choose to dress the table in a variety of ways, such as simply putting a tablecloth on it. To spruce up the process, try using different tablecloths or placemats at times throughout the week (or no mats or cloth at all for a sparse, clean look). You can also rotate or mix the style of dishes you use. How else can you enhance the space? Begin by identifying one item you would like to use. Light a fragrant candle, dim or brighten the lights, use various combinations of utensils and napkin holders, put on background music, or simply set out a vase of flowers. How about gathering colorful tree leaves and placing them around each person's place setting or putting an assortment of colored glass rocks you collected at the beach in a clear container in the center of the table? Why not select a piece of art, such as one your child created at summer camp, as a centerpiece? Consider whether the table is a shape that facilitates easy and equal conversation. Place photographs or art that reflect your family's tastes on the walls, or hang photos of dinners you've spent with a guest of honor. The most important thing is to create a welcoming atmosphere that represents the people who share meals there.

Have fun brainstorming ideas to personalize your eating space. A family I know painted their names on a white dining table to mark each member's respective seat. I recently painted my dining room chairs a lavender color and reupholstered the seat cushions using different fabric patterns on each chair. Why not? Let what you like dictate your decorating choices.

I've enjoyed giving platters to friends and family members for Christmas gifts or other occasions. I visit a paint-your-own pottery shop and create something customized for the recipient. My in-laws grow roses, so I painted a platter with a pink rose in the center. For my niece and her husband, I used the colors they chose for their wedding party. For my sister-in-law Bonnie and her husband, Tim, I used a soothing turquoise color that reminds me of their beautiful home. It's a great feeling to know that the platters I created for them will be used at future meals.

If you're a single person or part of a couple, think about what setting would work best for you given what you like and have on hand. You don't need matching items for your table to look appealing. In fact, it's sometimes more interesting when things don't match.

If you're part of a family, allow the family member who is responsible for setting the table to decide what tableware to use. If you have china, don't hesitate to use it every day if that's what feels right. Why wait for a holiday? Any shared meal is a special occasion.

If children are setting the table, encourage them to use whatever decorative items appeal to them. When my daughter was young, she decorated a dining room by tying balloons she had received from a friend's birthday party to each person's chair and placed an orange light bulb (leftover from Halloween) in a lamp she set on the table. For one birthday gathering, my daughter requested everyone wear red clothing (her favorite color). The beauty of letting kids use their imaginations is you will all enjoy some really fun ideas, and the kids will feel proud of their contributions.

During holiday meals with a large group of people, I sometimes print out menus, giving each dish a custom name. My stepmother-in-law, Pat, gets credit for this idea and for coming up with names such as *Potatoes Noel Bon Bon*, prepared by my sister-in-law Bonnie. Pat would print the menus in festive fonts on stationery and place a menu at each person's table setting. When my daughter Jini was twelve, she made a holiday appetizer we called *PepperonJini's*, which consisted of cream cheese and pepperoncini peppers rolled into slices of salami. She was thrilled to see her name and appetizer on the menu. Printed menus can easily make any meal event seem extra special, such as an anniversary or a meal welcoming a new neighbor.

Whatever your decisions in the design of your dining space, the experience will surely be enhanced by what you create.

Exercise: Too Many Cooks

There are many roles in planning and preparing shared meals.

During the planning stage for your shared-meal practice, hand out sheets of paper listing all of the roles involved in your plan. Some roles might include recipe researcher, shopper, vegetable chopper, cook, table setter, decorator, table clearer, and dishwasher filler. Use whatever titles you decide. Together, review all of the roles listed and discover if any are missing. Then ask each person to write his name at the top of the sheet.

Ask everyone to number the roles in order of preference, with the number one being the most enjoyable. Then ask them to share their top and bottom choices. Make it clear that everyone will get a chance to fill the roles they want but will be expected to volunteer to do the other ones at some point too. Encourage each member to think of one positive thing about his least desirable role. For example, a positive statement about dish washing might be that it is relaxing to have your hands in warm, soapy water.

Keep these lists when planning your meals for the week. Try to arrange the meal schedule so that once a week each person gets to fill his favorite role. Check in with your meal partners and ask if their preferences have changed, encouraging everyone to reconsider options they might have overlooked at first.

Step 7

Making Shared Meals a Sustainable Habit

We are what we repeatedly do. Excellence, then, is not an act, but a habit.
—Aristotle

Feel the Joy

At the heart of sustaining a shared-meal practice is realizing we need to integrate joy into our lives each day.

Just as our bodies are products of what we eat, our lives are products of the choices we've made. When we choose to spend time gathering around a table enjoying good food and company, we are choosing a lifestyle that promotes balance and harmony and celebrates the beauty of being in the moment. As we keep our shared-meal ritual going strong, we may find that other aspects of our lives fall into balance too.

Sometimes finding ways to feel joy arises out of simple ideas. The Italians have an ideal they aspire to called *l'arte d'arrangiarsi*, or "the art of making something out of nothing." Make a shared-meal "something" by using ordinary items you already have in your home. It's easy to elevate an experience into something special by putting forth even the tiniest effort. For a last-minute meal I shared with a special man, I found some glitter leftover from a birthday party to sprinkle around a white tablecloth. I lit a large candle in the center of the table, and the reflections from the glitter created delicate patterns on the dining room walls. I served a simple dish of spaghetti and meatballs, but my boyfriend expressed that this "extraordinary" meal made him feel extra special.

Often when my son and I share a meal, we'll look for some small way to make the meal special. When we shared a very basic meal of shepherd's pie, we drank sparking apple cider from beautiful wine glasses to add style. When you begin a shared-meal routine, you'll see how natural it is to craft something special out of what you previously considered ordinary. Your fun experiences will inspire you to find new ways to enhance future meals, and this will help sustain your practice.

I have two especially joyful memories about past shared meals and rituals in my family. During my childhood, whenever we learned a visitor was coming to dinner, someone would call out in response, "Get the Entenmann's!"—a box of pastries kept in a certain spot on the counter next to the refrigerator, just for such special occasions. Hearing the familiar call meant we'd soon be enjoying the company of a special guest. As a kid, it was exciting to speculate with my brothers and sisters about who the mystery person might be.

When John and Jini were young, I created a breakfast sandwich we named the *Egg McMama*. I used better ingredients than the famous fast-food chain and served them on mornings when there was a big exam. My son had heard that fatty foods, such as cheese and butter, improve cognitive brain performance. I wanted to show them we could make our own (slightly) healthier, homemade versions of this sandwich. Today, whenever my son or daughter requests an *Egg McMama*, it carries a lot of meaning—warm memories of school-day mornings sharing breakfast, joking about how much better their test grades would be. The added benefit was that having a few laughs before we left the house lightened the mood and reduced any anxiety they might have had over taking the test. I looked forward to the dinnertime report that night about the events of the school day, hoping to hear the special egg sandwich "did the trick."

You will see that once you start on the path of enjoying a shared-meal plan, you will create many joyful associations along the way and cultivate long-lasting memories.

Sustaining any habit also requires that we look at how we emotionally regulate ourselves when faced with daily choices—such as a short-term fix or a long-term benefit. It's easy to see how sharing meals can be overlooked in our efficient, instant-gratification world. We need only to remind ourselves that there are plenty of reasons to invest in the small amount of work necessary to sustain a shared-meal ritual. An attitude of mindfulness helps us to stay on track.

Researchers Aparna Labroo and Anirban Mukhopadhyay say our moods are malleable and can be changed by what we tell ourselves in the moment. They report that negative moods tend to be fleeting, while positive moods tend to be stable. And because many people feel compelled to act upon what they might not realize is a temporary feeling of negativity, they will seek a quick solution to correct it. For example, exhausted after finishing a twelve-hour day of work and errands, someone might decide to cancel dinner plans with friends and instead opt for the short-term fix of eating a microwave meal alone. Conversely, someone else who has the belief that a negative mood is only a temporary state may be more inclined to wait out any negative feelings of being too tired and continue with the plan to share dinner with friends, thus preserving the long-term benefit.

Maintaining change requires us to keep doing what caused improvement in the first place. It's a choice we make each time we decide what we'll do to support our practices. Lasting change calls for us to integrate what we're learning along the way too. Revel in the inspiration from the best ideas and practices you create and just don't worry about the rest.

As I've shared throughout this book, my personal practice of sharing meals has been, and continues to be, very positive. Because it's been so positive, I have a great deal of incentive to continue. However, sharing meals is not magical in and of itself; it does not automatically produce good results. If you do it carelessly, it can have detrimental effects. Thankfully, there are ways to minimize the possibility of any shadows marring the experience.

The Mealtime Environment

Along with the physical quality of the shared-meal environment, the social quality is extremely important. This fact was made clear to me in the study I performed of my childhood family meal ritual. During the interviews, I was quite surprised to learn that there was a difference in certain aspects of the social environment between my oldest and youngest siblings.

The five oldest siblings, who grew up during the forties and fifties, said they enjoyed family meals whenever meals included members of our extended family. They recalled a less enjoyable experience when they were dining only with immediate family members. This is because dialogue during these meals was regulated; children were expected to speak only when asked a question. Sometimes disciplining a child (or children) would seep into the mealtime. Fortunately, my parents' leadership style relaxed significantly over the decades and created a better and better experience as each year passed.

The six youngest siblings (including myself)—who grew up in the sixties, seventies, and early eighties—had consistently better experiences. Our gatherings were joyful, relaxed, and open, and conversation was shared by everyone. There were times when my parents made an incidental remark about a topic they wanted to address, but these times were infrequent, and I don't recall these comments spoiling the mood.

As mentioned earlier, my parents were influenced by parenting standards of their time. I have no doubt that they loved each of us dearly and cared for us to the best of their ability. I believe all parents do the best they can. Having a family meal ritual can help make the awesome task of raising children a little easier and bring couples closer together. A fifty-year study showed an association between family rituals and happier marriages. My parents' marriage showed improvement over the years too. In part, I attribute this to the bond they created by sustaining a shared-meal ritual for almost forty years.

I mention the differences in my siblings' experiences again to emphasize the point that even when shared meals are the norm in a household, the benefits can be reduced or negated if mealtime is an exercise in discipline. It's so important to resist the temptation to use time at the table to scold or lecture your kids or other family members.

Standards around the table should be considerate of everyone. The oldest of our siblings remembers with a certain amount of uneasiness the nonnegotiable clean-your-plate rule that was common during the forties and fifties. Some families may still practice this rule. Alan Lake, an associate professor of pediatrics at the Johns Hopkins University School of Medicine, advises against having your children eat everything on their plate. He says: "Parents should choose when to eat and what to eat, while a child should choose when to stop."

Maintaining a warm, relaxed and friendly environment is one of the single most important characteristics of a successful shared-meal practice. In many households today, this is a tall order because of the number of activities taking place simultaneously. However, it is possible to create the environment you want for your shared meals by following the strategies in this book. Using the exercises at the end of each chapter can also help bring a fresh set of experiences to your table. The bottom line is you must pay attention to the environment if you want to receive the benefits. *Quality counts.*

Some people wonder about the duration of each meal. Aim for each meal to last up to an hour—or longer if people want to linger. As you put your plan together, you and your partners will discover what feels natural. If your ritual is so relaxed that you continue to sit around the table for an extended period of time, just be sure that you are not eating more food merely because you are sitting there longer. Savor your food rather than rushing, and you shouldn't have a problem.

Some techniques for savoring your food are to take notice of how the food looks and appreciate the variety, color, and beauty of the ingredients. As you take each bite, notice the flavor differences, as well as the texture. Appreciate the ways your senses are stimulated. As you eat in a relaxed manner, this will help moderate your digestion, help you to feel satisfied by what you ate, and promote peacefulness, all of which lead you to an overall sense of well-being.

As mentioned throughout this book, the conversation at the table is also very important. To encourage easy conversation, invite everyone at the table to relax and take their time. There's no need to rush into conversation. If you or your companions are new to sharing meals or are out of practice with having in-person conversation, write a few topics on slips of paper and put them into a bowl on the table. Whenever the conversation lags, pull out a new topic.

The following are some possible topics (see more under Conversation Starters, Appendix G):

- Thorns and Roses: Each person takes a turn describing the high point of their day (the rose) and something challenging that happened (the thorn).

- Share about a book you've read lately and what you liked about it.
- Tell a joke—one that is appropriate for any age.
- Talk about your favorite movie, song, band, sports team, or subject at school.
- Name one thing you learned during the day.
- List your five favorite movies and describe why you like them.
- Talk about something that surprised you recently.
- Discuss your favorite television special or episode and why you liked it.
- Talk about a place you'd like to visit and why.
- Talk about someone you'd like to meet and why.
- Discuss your favorite color and your reason for choosing it.
- Ask your fellow diners to come up with a question for everyone at the table to answer.
- Share a new word you learned recently and use it in a sentence or say what you like about the word.
- Play an ingredient guessing game and have fun trying to identify the name of the ingredient.

Holiday Meals

Many people I've spoken with over the years talk about the joy they feel when sharing holiday meals, but they don't seem to be able to replicate these warm feelings for nonholiday meals. It seems they don't give themselves permission to experience this kind of joy outside of predetermined dates on a calendar.

What is it about holiday meals that make them special? A holiday meal doesn't seem to feel like a chore to most people. It has a feeling of ceremony, because those gathered have planned in advance to be present. In most families, everyone feels welcomed, and the air is filled with anticipation. The mood is lighthearted. Along with special dishes, there are lights, candles, music, and decorations. Plenty of hands prepare and serve the food, and it's common for people to volunteer to help. People generally arrive with positive feelings and don't waste precious time bringing up confrontational subjects. The ground rules for holiday meals are understood. People try to be on their best behavior and express gratitude for the efforts they each took to be together.

When building your practice, keep in mind the cooperative spirit that is typically present for holiday meals and let these qualities serve as a model for you as you shape your shared-meal plan.

Sharing Responsibility

Men anpil chay pa lou. (Many hands lighten the load.)
—Haitian proverb

Although making shared meals a sustainable habit requires some effort, there is no reason one person should go it alone. In fact, the attempt to "do it all" is detrimental to your health. By overloading yourself, you deny other people the chance to feel valued, be part of the team, and perhaps to learn a new skill.

Traditionally, women have had a difficult time opening their kitchens to others. On a trip to Florida, several of my sisters and I visited our sister Myra. We spent time making and sharing meals, some inspired by our childhood meals together. Early in our visit, we sensed Myra's slight possessiveness of her kitchen and teased her about it until she let us squeeze our way in to help more with the meals. We told her we just wanted a "piece of the action." Myra's attitude was understandable. Like many women growing up in the fifties, she feels particularly empowered in her kitchen, so it's no surprise she protects her space. It's where she has created wonderful meals—and I know this firsthand, having visited her frequently.

It's time to encourage women to find power in additional places. Open your kitchen! Make it an equal-opportunity environment. By getting more people involved, you'll be creating buy-in from everyone.

Involving others, especially kids, also brings about fun surprises in the kitchen. Years ago, my daughter and I found a recipe in a children's cookbook that combined thin spaghetti with strawberries and cottage cheese, rather than the more traditional tomato sauce and parmesan cheese. My kids and I watched curiously as the strawberry juice and cottage cheese combined to create a pink sauce. We agreed it was different, and we enjoyed eating it, although we also admitted we might not make it too often in the future. It was easier to get my kids involved in future meals because we had this fun experience together.

Another time my son asked if he could elaborate on his hot dog fixings. He added mayonnaise, whipped cream, jelly, and peanut butter, in addition to the traditional mustard and ketchup. It was amusing to watch him taste these combined flavors. John enjoyed that he was in control of his food choices, and the experiment sparked a conversation about using nontraditional ingredients too. By allowing children room to explore during mealtime activities, you capture their attention. This encourages them to take center stage in the action and look forward to the next time they can provide helping hands.

Leadership

The voice of parents is the voice of gods, for to their children, they are heaven's lieutenants.
—William Shakespeare

The importance of leadership in a shared-meal practice cannot be overstated.

Think about all you have read in this book and about what really matters to you in your everyday life. If you have a vision for your life to be a certain way, take the first step. Sometimes it takes just one person to start making changes that benefit and create inspiration for others around them.

Family therapist Ellyn Satter suggests that the practices you keep when feeding your child are vital to the love he feels from you. She emphasizes the role of the parent as critical. She says, "For your child's eating to turn out well, you must have a family table."

Children figure out what matters by observing what goes on in the home. Parents (and other caregivers) set the tone, and children understand the importance of shared meals in direct relation to their parents' behavior. If a parent acts with appreciation and warmth when his child passes the bowl of green beans, he will understand that his parent values him, the meal, and the time they are sharing.

Children need to see living examples of planning and preparing meals in order to develop their skills. Rest assured that your child won't fall apart if asked to help. In fact, you are neglecting your children's needs if you don't teach them how to make food for themselves. They'll need these skills when they begin to live independently so they don't exist on an unhealthy diet of processed food.

Contemporary parenting does not have the same structure as it did when I was growing up, but children (despite whatever they may say) still look to their parents for leadership.

It is up to parents and other caregivers to establish a shared-meal practice and to find ways to draw children back to the table, taking into account their own parenting styles and their children's personalities. Researchers at the University of Minnesota concluded that an authoritative style of parenting is best for increasing the frequency of family meals. The researchers defined authoritative parents as "Parents who were empathic and respectful, but who maintained clear boundaries and expectations."

Some children will help plan and prepare meals simply because their parents require it. Children of all ages understand requirements. They get up, get dressed, go to school, take exams, groom themselves, do their homework, and meet many other expectations given to them. Having standards for sharing meals shouldn't be too much of a hurdle to overcome if you present them as a normal part of everyday life.

The same concept holds true if you are part of a couple or single. When you decide to move ahead with your shared-meal plan, regard it as an updated feature of daily life, and you will influence others to do the same.

I hope my research, stories, and exercises have inspired you to join *The Shared-Meal Revolution*, and you have learned how sharing meals offers a multitude of rich benefits. Once your practice is established, the rewards will encourage you to continue—as long as you uphold high standards of behavior and focus on being in the moment, fully present, and enjoying the experience.

Although at times in this book I've emphasized the importance of meals for families, the benefits of sharing meals extend to each and every person in our American society. It's what we *all* need to live our best lives. When we share meals, we are actively reclaiming necessary balance, which will help us to feel more alive and refreshed each and every day.

You don't have to settle for a life that feels detached from others. You don't have to just wish you could have a more whole and engaging home life. You have a new awareness of how the simple, sweet act of sharing a meal can brighten your life. It's time for you to discover how much more meaningful your life can feel when you are truly connected with others.

When you take the lead, you will help create lifelong experiences you and your loved ones will treasure for a lifetime. What more precious a gift could we give to one another than one that promises an enduring legacy of love?

Not unlike many goals in life, if sharing meals required no effort, most people would be doing it already. Remember, it's the reward that makes any pursuit worthwhile. When you create a plan that's right for you, it won't feel like work. It will be a natural, joyous part of living.

I am confident that as a loving and caring American society, we are up to the challenge.

Exercise: The Fruits of Your Labors

Many people benefit seeing the progress they have made over a long period of time. Although I encourage you to keep up your practice of frequent progress checks, you might benefit from performing this exercise.

Right now, write down what you feel is the single most important aspect of sharing meals. If you can, write one word that sums up this aspect. Date the paper and seal it in an envelope. Put it in a place you will remember. Set a calendar reminder to look at it one year from now.

As you proceed during this year of sharing meals, reflect on the other areas of your life that have been affected positively by your decision to make sharing meals a priority. Using a journal you have reserved for the purpose of shared-meal thoughts and ideas, write some of these positive changes in as much detail as you can.

Think about the empowerment you feel as a result of getting better at designing and preparing meals. Describe three ways in which you have improved in these areas.

After one year has passed, locate the envelope you had put away at the start of your new shared-meal practice. Open it and read what you wrote a year ago to describe the single most important aspect of sharing meals. Is it still accurate? Reflect on how your perspective has changed (or perhaps, stayed the same). On the same piece of paper, write a second word that describes which aspect of the shared-meal experience is most important to you now, one year later. Plan to recheck this piece of paper once a year to see how your attitudes and experiences about sharing meals are evolving.

APPENDICES

Appendix A

Frequency Survey

This survey is to be used to capture how many times a week you are currently sharing meals with others. Please put a √ mark next to the meal you shared with at least one family member or friend.

Try this survey for two consecutive 7-day cycles. Review how many times, what days of the week, and what meal type you enjoyed with someone else.

Week #1 (Dates) ____	Meals: B = Breakfast; L= Lunch; D = Dinner *Please put a check (√) next to the meal(s) that you have with your family or friends.*
Sunday	B=_____ L=_____ D=_____
Monday	B=_____ L=_____ D=_____
Tuesday	B=_____ L=_____ D=_____
Wednesday	B=_____ L=_____ D=_____
Thursday	B=_____ L=_____ D=_____
Friday	B=_____ L=_____ D=_____
Saturday	B=_____ L=_____ D=_____

Week #2 (Dates) ____	Meals: B = Breakfast; L= Lunch; D = Dinner *Please put a check (√) next to the meal(s) that you have with your family or friends.*
Sunday	B=_____ L=_____ D=_____
Monday	B=_____ L=_____ D=_____
Tuesday	B=_____ L=_____ D=_____
Wednesday	B=_____ L=_____ D=_____
Thursday	B=_____ L=_____ D=_____
Friday	B=_____ L=_____ D=_____
Saturday	B=_____ L=_____ D=_____

Appendix B

Activity Chart: Who's Doing What When?

Week of _____:

Preparation
    Planning menus:
    Shopping for groceries:

Cooking
    Head or lead chef:
    Assistant or sous-chef:

The Event
    Announcing the meal is ready to be served:
    Setting the table:
    Mood maker (music, lighting, candles):

The After-Party
    Announcing/marking the conclusion of the meal:
    Clearing the table:
    Kitchen cleanup:

Appendix C

Project Plan and Spiritual Ritual Plan Examples:

Use one of the following two examples to make a template for your own shared-meal plan. (You can read more about these ideas in Step 6.)

Example 1: Project Plan (See Step 6.)

Vision statement (describes the guiding image of your shared-meal plan's success):

_____
_____

Mission statement (describes the specific activities that will achieve your vision):

_____
_____

Values (describes the characteristics that underlie the vision):

_____
_____

Short-term objectives (describes one or more immediate goals):

_____
_____

Long-term objectives (describes the goals that will take longer to achieve and are wider in scope than the short-term objective):

_____
_____

Action plan (describes a set of specific steps to help you achieve your objectives):

_____

_____

Strategy evaluation (describes how you will assess if your plan is on course):

_____

_____

Performance measurement (describes how you will measure the performance of those in your plan):

_____

_____

Corrective action (describes how you will change methods and performance to get on course for fulfilling your goals):

_____

_____

Example 2: Spiritual Ritual Plan (See Step 6.)

Grounding: As the leader of the ritual, you agree to host the first shared meal. You set the tone by offering your commitment to a calm and loving shared-meal practice.

_____

_____

Sacred Space: You discuss locations and decide where your shared-meal ritual will take place. Before each meal, free the space of distraction in order to promote peaceful feelings and positive energy.

_____

_____

Tools: Consider what physical materials you will need to create a meaningful shared-meal ritual.

_____

_____

Intention: An agreement is made to set the intention to ensure the best possible shared-meal experience.

_____

_____

The Heart: During the meal, we will honor those gathered around the table.

_____

_____

Closing/Give Thanks: As you conclude the shared meal, offer thanks.

_____

_____

Appendix D

Pantry Staples

Customize the following list to suit your needs and tastes.

Oils (olive, vegetable, canola, peanut, sesame)
Vinegars (balsamic, sherry, red wine, apple cider, champagne, white distilled)
Rice (brown, white, long-grain, Arborio, quinoa)
Beans (any variety, including black, chick/garbanzo, kidney, lentils)
Pastas (whole-grain, whole wheat, brown rice, spinach, egg)
Broths (chicken, beef, vegetable)
Condiments or sauces (soy, teriyaki, barbeque, curry, honey, mustard, mayonnaise)
Fruits (lemon, lime, apples, pears, oranges, pomegranate)
Nuts (variety, including almonds, pine nuts, cashews, pecans)
Spices (variety, including paprika, cayenne, curry, paprika, turmeric)
Dried and fresh herbs (bay leaves, oregano, parsley, chives, mint, rosemary, thyme, sage)
Baking products (baking soda, baking powder, cornstarch, cornmeal)
Sugar (unrefined, white, raw, brown)
Flour (variety, including all-purpose, cake flour, whole-wheat)
Extracts (vanilla, lemon, almond, anise)

Appendix E

Build-a-Meal Template

You can quickly and easily plan countless meals by following the steps below.

Step 1: Choose a Carbohydrate
- Pasta (spinach, whole grain, brown rice, etc.)
- Potatoes (sweet, red, yellow, russet, etc.) or yams
- Rice (brown, white, jasmine, basmati, etc.)
- Beans (cannellini, black, lentils, etc.) or peas
- Quinoa
- Other _____

Step 2: Choose a Protein
- Beef
- Turkey
- Chicken
- Pork
- Ham
- Veggie patty
- Tofu
- Egg or egg whites
- Other _____

Step 3: Choose a Vegetable
- Leafy greens
- Zucchini
- Broccoli
- Spinach
- Beets
- Carrots
- Tomatoes
- Onions
- Cabbage

- Eggplant
- Cucumbers
- Avocados
- Mushrooms
- Other _____

Step 4 (optional): Choose a Sauce
- Tomato
- Pesto
- Mushroom gravy
- White/creamy
- Barbecue
- Curry
- Chutney
- Ranch
- Salsa
- Tzatziki
- Ginger/soy
- Other _____

Step 5: Choose a Fruit
- Berries
- Grapes
- Oranges
- Kiwis
- Melon
- Other _____

Step 6: Choose a "Dairy" Product
- Milk (reduced-fat, almond, soy, rice)
- Yogurt
- Cheese (goat, feta, blue, parmesan, etc.)
- Other _____

Appendix F

Recipes, Cooking Skills, and Related Resources

The Food Network website (http://www.foodnetwork.com) and the Cooking Channel (http://www.cookingchanneltv.com) have vast resources for recipes. One area I like is by Chef Kelsey Nixon. She offers a lot of very useful, basic information about cooking skills at: http://www.cookingchanneltv.com/kelsey-nixon/index.html.

Chef Rachael Ray has several helpful shows for people planning and preparing meals. Here's one of my favorites: http://www.cookingchanneltv.com/rachael-rays-week-in-a-day/index.html.

KitchenCue is a comprehensive DVD cooking series to help you in all facets of meal preparation: http://www.kitchencue.com.

Other Internet resources for recipes are: http://www.recipesource.com, http://www.allrecipes.com, http://www.epicurious.com, http://www.bonappetit.com, and http://www.food.com.

In Jamie Oliver's book *Jamie Oliver's Meals in Minutes* (Penguin Press, 2011, page 21), he offers what he calls The List of kitchen equipment.

http://www.foodreference.com. FoodReference.com offers educational information and trivia about food.

This website offers a variety of health and wellness tips and research from leading experts around the world: http://www.sharecare.com.

Appendix G

Conversation Starters

Here are some additional conversation starters (see more in Step 7).
- Who is, or was, your favorite teacher and why?
- Name a new sport you would like to try and why.
- Describe the most exciting moment of your life.
- What is your earliest memory from childhood?
- If you could have chosen your own name, would it be the same as your current name? If not, what would it be?
- What was the proudest moment of your life so far?
- What new career would you choose if you could no longer continue in the one you have now?
- If you had to live somewhere for one month without any electronics, where would you want to be?

Appendix H

The Politics of Nutrition

The amount of inexpensive and highly processed food available in America is startling, and we can no longer deny the detrimental effects this can present to our health and the environment. Many families use these foods as staples in their diets because they cannot afford better quality food. We can all help change the state of the food industry by eating locally grown food whenever possible and by contacting our elected leaders to ask them for help. Ask them to support making healthy food available for everyone. Ask what legislation they are working on to support local farming. Tell them you want their help so you can always have access to reasonably priced, nutritious food (without harmful chemicals) that allows you to stay within your family budget.

If your state does not already have legislation requiring fast-food chains and restaurants to provide printed nutritional information about the foods they serve, write to your representative in Congress and request this change.

The following resources provide more information and ideas discussed in the book around health and nutrition:

Alice Waters, The Edible Schoolyard (http://www.edibleschoolyard. org).

Jamie Oliver promotes supplying better food at school for kids and encourages them to develop better eating habits: http://www. jamieoliver.com/us/foundation/jamies-food-revolution/sign-petition.

Mark Bittman, author and food columnist, promotes "flexitarian" eating leading to better health and protecting our natural resources (http://www.markbittman.com).

Author and food activist Michael Pollan (http://www.michaelpollan. com) regularly writes and lectures about the topics of food agriculture, health, and the environment.

The partnership between the Clinton Foundation and the American Heart Association promotes better nutrition for children (http:// www.healthiergeneration.org).

Led by First Lady Michelle Obama, Let's Move is America's campaign to help children reach adulthood at a healthy weight (http://www. letsmove.gov).

Rachael Ray's nonprofit organization, Yum-O!, promotes healthy eating and getting kids into the kitchen (http://www.yum-o.org).

The Slow Food Movement encourages healthy, relaxed eating and a responsibility to the environment (http://www.slowfoodusa.org).

Dr. David L. Katz is President and Founder of Turn the Tide foundation, a nonprofit organization focusing on practical programs to combat the obesity epidemic: http://www.turnthetidefoundation.org.

One in five American children struggles with hunger. Share Our Strength's *No Kid Hungry* campaign is ending childhood hunger in America. Contact them for more information and ways to help. (http://www.nokidhungry.org).

Notes

Introduction

p. xx. Industrialization spurred a movement away: Lynn Spigel, *Make Room for TV: Television and the Family Ideal in Postwar America* (Chicago: University of Chicago Press, 1992), 12.

p. xx. Changes in the workforce offered these new urban workers: Charles L. Harper and Bryan F. Le Beau, *Food, Society, and Environment* (Upper Saddle River, NJ: Prentice Hall, 2003), 63.

p. xx. took advantage of convenient solutions: Ibid., 86–87.

p. xx. the fast-food craze: Ibid., 102–103.

p. xx. Food delivery services: Ibid.

p. xxi. deskfast: Paul Roberts, *The End of Food* (New York: Houghton Mifflin, 2008), 44.

p. xxi. al desko: Ibid.

p. xxi. expanding appetite for snack foods: Ibid. According to Roberts, a highly profitable, highly processed snack food industry is hard at work to bring products to the market that "can be consumed one-handed" while not causing a mess. The appeal behind these snack products is that they won't slow down interaction with handheld electronic devices or cause an individual to slow down his work production.

p. xxii. Where's the soul?: I am inspired by the Slow Food movement, which endorses using local food, respecting the environment where food is grown and produced, and enjoying a relaxed, shared dining experience. The Slow Food culture started to simmer in Italy in 1986 and has been gaining momentum internationally ever since. See Carl Honoré, *In Praise of Slowness: How a Worldwide Movement Is Challenging the Cult of Speed* (New York: HarperCollins, 2004), 59.

p. xxii. For eating is the most basic interaction: Paul Roberts, "The New Food Anxiety," *Psychology Today* (March 1, 1998): http://www. psychologytoday.com/articles/199803/the-new-food-anxiety.

p. xxii. Eating with others transforms biological hunger: Harper and Le Beau, *Food, Society, and Environment,* 131.

p. xxiii. food cultures that once treated cooking: Paul Roberts, *The End of Food* (New York: Houghton Mifflin, 2008), xii.

p. xxiii. grill marks: Ibid., 43.

p. xxiii. The genius marketing of these food products: Ibid., 42–43.

p. xxiii. spiritual anorexia: Leon Kass quoted in Paul Roberts, "The New Food Anxiety," *Psychology Today* (March 1, 1998): http://www. psychologytoday.com/articles/199803/the-new-food-anxiety.

p. xxiii. still eat when hungry, but no longer know what it means: Ibid.

Step 1: Understanding the Significance of Shared Meals

p. 2. being together as a family: Carol Archambeault, "Family Meals: A Multigenerational Perspective on the Developmental Impact of the Family Meal Ritual" (master's thesis, Pacific Oaks College, December 2007), 115–16. *Author's note*: Throughout this book, pseudonyms were used in place of my siblings' real names when referencing comments from the master's thesis.

p. 3. attention deficit disorder: Ibid., 109.

p. 3. versus becoming overly self-involved: Ibid.

p. 3. increase in the divorce rate and more women in the workforce: Ibid., 98.

p. 3. parents today have less talent: Ibid.

p. 3. talking to your kids about drugs: Ibid.

p. 3. We need a witness to our lives: "The Rumba," *Shall We Dance,* directed by Peter Chelsom, (2004; Santa Monica, CA: Miramax Films), DVD.

p. 3. healthy nutrition: Mary Story and Jamie Stang, "Understanding Adolescent Eating Behaviors" in *Guidelines for Adolescent Nutrition Services,* (Minneapolis: Center for Leadership, Education, and Training in Maternal and Child Nutrition, Division of Epidemiology and Community Health, School of Public Health, University of Minnesota, 2005), chapter 2, page 15: http://www.epi.umn.edu/let/pubs/adol_book.shtm.

p. 3. healthy nutrition: Nicole Larson, Dianne Neumark-Sztainer, Peter J. Hannan, and Mary Story, "Family Meals during Adolescence Are Associated with Higher Diet Quality and Healthful Meal Patterns during Young Adulthood," *Journal of the American Dietetic Association* 107, no. 9 (September 2007): 1502–1510.

p. 3. healthy nutrition: Randi Hutter Epstein, "Linking Children's Health to Family Meals," *New York Times*, March 28, 2000, http://www.nytimes.com/2000/03/28/health/linking-children-s-health-to-family-meals.html?sec=health.

p. 3. strong social skills and cohesiveness: James H. S. Bossard, "Family Table Talk: An Area for Sociological Study," *American Sociological Review* 8, no. 3 (June 1943): 295–297.

p. 3. strong social skills and cohesiveness: Jeffrey Kluger, Christine Gorman, and Alice Park, "America's Obesity Crisis: Eating Behavior: Why We Eat," *Time*, June 7, 2004, 72.

p. 3. positive emotional and mental health: Marla Eisenberg, Rachel Olson, Dianne Neumark-Sztainer, Mary Story, and Linda Bearinger, "Correlations Between Family Meals and Psychosocial Well-Being Among Adolescents," *Archives of Pediatrics and Adolescent Medicine* 158, no. 8 (August 2004): 795.

p. 3. positive emotional and mental health: The Friedman School of Science and Policy, "Families That Eat Together," *Tufts University Health & Nutrition Letter* 15 (October 1997): 2–3.

p. 3. positive academic performance in adolescents: The National Center on Addiction and Substance Abuse at Columbia University, "The Importance of Family Dinners," September 2003: 6.

p. 3. positive academic performance in adolescents: The National Center on Addiction and Substance Abuse at Columbia University, "The Importance of Family Dinners II," September 2005: 11.

p. 3. positive academic performance in adolescents: The National Center on Addiction and Substance Abuse at Columbia University, "The Importance of Family Dinners V," September 2009: 2.

p. 3. stronger family relationships: "The Importance of Family Dinners II," 9.

p. 3. stronger family relationships: "The Importance of Family Dinners V," 8–9.

p. 3. happier marriages: "Family Meals Lead to Healthy and Happy Children," *Bristol Evening Post*, December 10, 2002.

p. 3. deeper connection to ethnic and cultural identity: Nancy Gibbs, "The Magic of the Family Meal," *Time*, June 4, 2006, 1, http://www.time.com/time/magazine/article/0,9171,1200760,00.html.

p. 3. deeper connection to ethnic and cultural identity: James H. S. Bossard, "Family Table Talk: An Area for Sociological Study," *American Sociological Review* 8, no. 3 (June 1943): 298–301.

p. 4. enhanced feelings of spirituality: Gibbs, "The Magic of the Family Meal," 1.

p. 4. enhanced feelings of spirituality: Alice Waters, "The Ethics of Eating (Part 2)," *Whole Earth 90* (Summer 1997): 64–65.

p. 4. reduced risky behaviors and substance abuse in teens: "The Importance of Family Dinners," 3–11.

p. 4. reduced risky behaviors and substance abuse in teens: "The Importance of Family Dinners II," 3–11.

p. 4. reduced risky behaviors and substance abuse in teens: "The Importance of Family Dinners V," 3–7.

p. 4. relationship with their parents as fair or poor: Ibid., 8.

p. 4. they have excellent relationships: Ibid.

p. 5. more likely to have access to drugs: Ibid., 5.

p. 5. The family meal teaches children about behavior in a social group: Steven J. Wolin quoted in Elizabeth G. Jackson, "Family Meals More Important than Nutritional Perfection," *Environmental Nutrition* 13, no. 9 (1990): 1.

p. 5. daily domestic life doesn't matter: Lionel Tiger quoted in E. Jackson, Ibid.

p. 5. highly processed heat-and-eat meals: Roberts, *The End of Food*, 42.

p. 5. In a Federal Trade Commission report: Federal Trade Commission, "Marketing Food to Children and Adolescents: A Review of Industry Expenditures, Activities, and Self-Regulation: A Report to Congress" (July 2008): ES-1, http://www.ftc.gov/os/2008/07/P064504foodmktingreport.pdf.

p. 6. one-person households: Jacqueline Olds and Richard S. Schwartz, *The Lonely American: Drifting Apart in the Twenty-first Century* (Boston: Beacon Press, 2009), 79.

p. 6. 28 percent of all households: Eric Klinenberg, "Living Alone Is the New Norm," *Time*, March 12, 2012, 60.

p. 6. social atomization: James Cote, *Arrested Adulthood: The Changing Nature of Maturity and Identity* (New York: New York University, 2000), 71.

p. 6. never spend a social evening with a neighbor: Robert Putnam quoted in Cote, *Arrested Adulthood*, 71.

p. 6. everyday conversation with another person: Ibid.

p. 6. If you belong to no groups but decide to join one: Robert Putnam, *Bowling Alone: The Collapse and Revival of American Community* (New York: Simon & Schuster, 2000), 331.

p. 6. Positive social relationships are second only to genetics: Olds and Schwartz, *The Lonely American*, 136.

p. 7. Erosion of social capital has measurable ill effects: Robert Putnam, *Bowling Alone: The Collapse and Revival of American Community* (New York: Simon & Schuster, 2000), 331.

p. 7. social exclusion: Olds and Schwartz, *The Lonely American*, 70.

p. 7. variety of self-defeating behaviors: Ibid., 72–73.

p. 7. avoids meaningful thought, emotion: Ibid., 73.

p. 7. give up and stop trying: Ibid., 73.

p. 7. dramatically changes how people function: Ibid., 73–74.

p. 7. perpetual tension between freedom and connection: Ibid., 12.

p. 7. People in our society drift away from social connections: Ibid., 11.

p. 8. Connection is why we're here: Brené Brown, "The Power of Vulnerability," video, 20:21, filmed at TEDxHouston in June 2010, http://www.ted.com/talks/brene_brown_on_vulnerability.html.

p. 8. You are not sure you are going to get a reward: Patricia Wallace quoted in Claudia Wallis, "The Multitasking Generation," *Time*, March 19, 2006, 6, http://www.time.com/time/magazine/article/0,9171,1174696,00.html.

p. 8. Rabbi Irwin Kula: Rabbi Irwin Kula, interview by Helen Whitney, "Faith and Doubt at Ground Zero," *Frontline*, Act 2, PBS, September 3, 2002, http://www.pbs.org/wgbh/pages/frontline/shows/faith/interviews/kula.html (December 28, 2011). This is a beautiful and thought-provoking documentary filled with deep insights from a variety of religious leaders and offers firsthand accounts of those involved with the September 11, 2001, tragedy.

p. 10. A worldwide Gallup poll: "Can Money Buy Happiness? Gallup Poll Asks, and the World Answers," *ScienceDaily.com*, July 2, 2010, http://www.sciencedaily.com/releases/2010/07/100701072652.htm. A Gallup World Poll conducted during 2005 and 2006 surveyed 136,000 people in 132 countries, asking respondents to rate their daily satisfaction in various areas of their lives. Researchers then analyzed their answers as they related to income and standard of living. The results indicate that "life satisfaction" does increase with increased income, but that other factors, including feeling control over one's own life, feeling respected, and having the social support one needs, influence happiness even more strongly.

p. 10. Once the basic necessities have been achieved: David Brooks, "The Sandra Bullock Trade," *New York Times*, March 29, 2010, http://www.nytimes.com/2010/03/30/opinion/30brooks.html.

p. 10. oriented around the things that are easy to count: Ibid.

p. 10. joining a group that meets even just once a month: Ibid.

p. 10. sex, socializing after work and having dinner with others: Ibid.

p. 11. half hour a day with your inner circle: Dan Buettner, *The Blue Zone: Lessons for Living Longer from the People Who've Lived the Longest*, (Washington, DC: National Geographic, 2008), 259.

p. 11. Make one family meal a day sacred: Ibid., 257.

Carol Archambeault

Step 2: Recognizing the Developmental Benefits of Shared Meals

(Part A)

p. 15. helps to develop children's social skills: James H. S. Bossard, "Family Table Talk," *American Sociological Review*, 297–298.

p. 15. personality clinic: Ibid., 298.

p. 15. Interaction over food is the single most important feature of socializing: Sidney Mintz in Jeffrey Kluger, Christine Gorman, and Alice Park, "America's Obesity Crisis: Eating Behavior: Why We Eat," *Time*, June 7, 2004, 1, http://www.time.com/time/magazine/article/0,9171,994388,00.html.

p. 16. my brother Ned said that interacting with a wide variety of personalities: Archambeault, "Family Meals," 93.

p. 16. My brother Tim added that it was a definite aid for speaking: Ibid.

p. 16. embraces other people more than other things: Russell Belk quoted in "Share and Share Alike," *ScienceDaily.com*, August 25, 2009, http://www.sciencedaily.com/releases/2009/08/090824182443.htm.

p. 16. individualization of family meals: Ibid.

p. 17. The senses are good at reading body language: Robert Bolton, PhD, *People Skills: How to Assert Yourself, Listen to Others, and Resolve Conflicts* (New York: Simon & Schuster, 1979), 78–84.

p. 17. orbitofrontal cortex: Olds and Schwartz, *The Lonely American*, 104.

p. 17. Sharing food with another human being is an intimate act: Mary Frances Kennedy Fisher, *The Art of Eating* (New York: Vintage Books, 1976), 577.

p. 17. sex and food are the two principal bonds: Naomichi Ishige, "Table Manners Makyth Man: The Emergence of Homo sapiens as Convivial Animal," *Unesco Courier*, May 1987, 18.

p. 18. kyoshoku shudan: Ibid.

p. 18. conviviality is a trait particular to the human race: Ibid.

p. 18. the family system should be protected through family meals: Ibid.

p. 18. the shared meal is a primal activity: Ibid.

p. 18. the one cheap pleasure that could ever rival sex: Paul Roberts, *The End of Food*, xii.

p. 18. We need to sit and talk about things: Archambeault, "Family Meals," 99.

p. 20. contemporary psychologist Daniel Goleman: Daniel Goleman, "What Is Social Intelligence?," Greater Good, Fall/Winter 2006–2007, http://greatergood.berkeley.edu/article/item/what_is_social_intelligence.

p. 20. Thorndike stresses the usefulness of these skills: Ibid.

p. 23. Data gathered by The Centers for Disease Control and Prevention (CDC): Centers for Disease Control and Prevention, "Adult Obesity: Obesity Rises among Adults," August 2010, http://www.cdc.gov/vitalsigns/AdultObesity. Obesity is defined by the CDC as a body mass index (BMI) of 30 or more.

p. 23. The CDC also reports that 17 percent: Centers for Disease Control and Prevention, "Childhood Overweight and Obesity," *National Health and Nutrition Examination Survey,* 2007–2008, http://www.cdc.gov/obesity/childhood.

p. 23. likely to suffer from more severe obesity as an adult: Ibid. Fortunately, many public figures and health organizations have taken the lead in addressing childhood obesity, such as the Bill Clinton Foundation and the American Heart Association, who have partnered to help fight obesity through their Alliance for a Healthy America; Dr. David L. Katz with his Turn the Tide Foundation; First Lady Michelle Obama with her Let's Move campaign; television personality and chef Rachel Ray with her nonprofit organization Yum-O!; and British chef Jamie Oliver with his television show and website *Jamie Oliver's Food Revolution.*

p. 23. We eat an alarming 40 percent: Paul Roberts, *The End of Food* (New York: Houghton Mifflin, 2008), 34.

p. 23. Most children don't meet the CDC's daily recommendations: The Centers for Disease Control and Prevention, under "Eating Behaviors of Young People," accessed April 15, 2013, http://www.cdc.gov/healthyyouth/nutrition/facts.htm.

p. 24. Certain factors seem to contribute to dietary composition: Mary Story and Jamie Stang, "Understanding Adolescent Eating Behaviors" in *Guidelines for Adolescent Nutrition Services*, chapter 2, page 12: http://www.epi.umn.edu/let/pubs/adol_book.shtm.

p. 24. Researchers at Project EAT: "Regular Family Meals Result in Better Eating Habits for Adolescents," *ScienceDaily.com*, March 10, 2009, 1–2, http://www.sciencedaily.com/releases/2009/03/090309104710.htm.

p. 24. frequency of family meals was down from 60 percent: Ibid.

p. 24. Researcher Teri L. Burgess-Champoux concluded: Ibid., 2.

p. 25. Another study conducted by the researchers at Project EAT: Nicole I. Larson, MPH, RD, Dianne Neumark-Sztainer, PhD, MPH, RD, Peter J. Hannan, MStat, and Mary Story, PhD, RD, "Family Meals during Adolescence Are Associated with Higher Diet Quality and Healthful Meal Patterns during Young Adulthood," *Journal of the American Dietetic Association* 107, no. 9 (September 2007): 1502–1510, http://www.journals.elsevierhealth.com/periodicals/yjada/article/ S0002-8223%2807%2901292-8/abstract.

p. 25. Five years later, at age twenty: Ibid.

p. 25. grade school kids who ate with their parents: Lori Nudo, "Make a Dinner Date Tonight! Sit-down Meals Feed Healthy Habits," *Prevention,* July 2002, 48.

p. 25. when parents select nutritious food in the presence of their children: Randi Hutter Epstein, "Linking Children's Health to Family Meals," *New York Times,* March 28, 2000, http://www.nytimes.com/2000/03/28/health/linking-children-s-health-to-family-meals.html?sec=health.

p. 26. eating slowly has the added benefit of allowing the brain: Honoré, *In Praise of Slowness,* 72.

p. 26. A study published in Psychological Science: Catherine Saint Louis, "Rituals Make Our Food More Flavorful," *New York Times,* August 9, 2013, http://well.blogs.nytimes.com/2013/08/09/rituals-make-our-food-more-flavorful/?hpw&_r=0.

p. 26. ritualized gestures: Ibid.

p. 26. involvement in the food: Ibid.

p. 26. Home needs to be the heart of passing on food culture: Jamie Oliver, "Teach Every Child About Food," video, 21:53, filmed at TED2010 in Long Beach, CA, in February 2010, http://www.ted.com/talks/jamie_oliver.html.

p. 26. Oliver also offers some wonderful programs to get kids in the kitchen: See http://www.jamieoliver.com/us/foundation/jamies-food-revolution/sign-petition and http://www.jamieoliver.com/foundation/about.

p. 27. growing up believing dessert: Archambeault, "Family Meals," 85.

p. 27. The average food item on a U.S. grocery shelf: Barbara Kingsolver, *Animal, Vegetable, Miracle* (New York: HarperCollins, 2007), 4. In this fascinating book, Kingsolver and her family embark on a one-year journey to rid themselves of industrialized food by eating food they grow themselves or only from local sources in the community in which they live.

p. 27. Popular food journalist Mark Bittman: Mark Bittman, *Food Matters: A Guide to Conscious Eating with More Than 75 Recipes* (New York: Simon & Schuster, 2009), 93.

p. 27. his recommendations of eating sanely: Ibid.

p. 28. Eat all the plants you can manage: Ibid. If you are feeling overwhelmed by the amount of dieting and nutrition information in the marketplace, consider looking at Bittman's wonderful book, which is full of recipes as well as straightforward information about food choices and the state of our food industry.

p. 30. household dynamic in which children feel secure and loved: The Friedman School of Science and Policy, "Families That Eat Together," *Tufts University Health & Nutrition Letter,* 15 (October 1997): 2–3.

p. 30. found a trend in mental health benefits: "In Case You Haven't Heard," *Mental Health Weekly* 12, no. 7 (February 18, 2002): 8.

p. 31. help your children have better relationships with their friends: The Friedman School of Science and Policy, "Families That Eat Together," *Tufts University Health & Nutrition Letter,* 15 (October 1997): 2–3.

p. 31. A 1987 study performed by psychiatrist Steven J. Wolin: Miriam Weinstein, *The Surprising Power of Family Meals: How Eating Together Makes Us Smarter, Stronger, Healthier and Happier* (Hanover: Steerforth, 2005), 38.

p. 31. alcoholic homes where rituals were held: Ibid., 43

p. 31. rituals offer a stabilizing effect: Ibid., 46

p. 32. Systems of communication that are considered open: Virginia Satir, *The New Peoplemaking* (Mountain View, CA: Science and Behavior Books, 1988), 135.

p. 32. develop their identities through food choices: Mary Story and Jamie Stang, "Understanding Adolescent Eating Behaviors" in *Guidelines for Adolescent Nutrition Services,* chapter 2, page 16: http://www.epi.umn.edu/let/pubs/adol_book.shtm.

p. 32. CASA reveals correlations between infrequent family dining and teenagers' ability: The National Center on Addiction and Substance Abuse at Columbia University, "The Importance of Family Dinners V," September 2009, 5.

p. 32. As reported by the National Eating Disorders Association (NEDA): National Eating Disorders Association, "Facts and statistics," accessed July 1, 2010, http://www.nationaleatingdisorders.org/information-resources/general-information.php#facts-statistics.

p. 33. at least three to four meals a week have less disordered eating: Dianne Neumark-Sztainer, PhD, *"I'm, Like, SO Fat!" Helping Your Teen Make Healthy Choices about Eating and Exercise in a Weight-Obsessed World* (New York: The Guilford Press, 2005), 194.

p. 33. routine family meals may provide some emotional protection for adolescents: Marla Eisenberg, Rachel Olson, Dianne Neumark-Sztainer, Mary Story, and Linda Bearinger, "Correlations between Family Meals and Psychosocial Well-Being Among Adolescents," *Archives of Pediatrics and Adolescent Medicine* 158, no. 8 (August 2004): 795.

p. 33. family connectedness: Ibid., 795.

p. 33. above and beyond their general sense of connection: Ibid., 795.

p. 34. young males start looking away from the family: Michael Gurian, *A Fine Young Man* (New York: Tarcher/Putnam, 1998), 141.

p. 34. routines in the household: Ibid.

p. 34. clan activity: Ibid.

p. 34. Protect your family rituals like they are gold: Ibid., 142.

p. 34. a high priority over other activities: Ibid., 141.

p. 34. When I was raising my children: Psychologist Carol Gilligan theorized that women regard their psychological development in strong relation with others, seeing the self and the other as "interdependent." According to Gilligan, there is a natural motivation and a mutual benefit for women to care for others through routines, because "the activity of care enhances both others and self." The shared-meal ritual provides such an opportunity. I do know that I received as much as I gave through maintaining the shared-meal ritual with my children. See Carol Gilligan, *In A Different Voice* (Cambridge, MA: Harvard University Press, 1993), 74.

p. 35. families who share dinners more frequently (at least five dinners per week) have less stress: The National Center on Addiction and Substance Abuse at Columbia University, "The Importance of Family Dinners II," September 2005, 9.

p. 35. Notable psychologist and author Frederic Hudson: Frederic M. Hudson, PhD, *The Adult Years: Mastering the Art of Self Renewal* (San Francisco: Jossey-Bass, 1999), 21.

p. 35. trying to remove the uncertainty: Ibid., 22.

p. 35. insulating ourselves in personal concerns: Ibid., 22.

p. 35. body, mind, and spirit: Ibid., 235.

p. 35. Hudson's ten qualities of self-renewal: Ibid., 235–241.

p. 36. who are ready to do more with their lives than merely succeed: Ibid., 27.

p. 36. Loss of appetite is one of the by-products: Tufts University, "For Senior Citizens Who Live Alone," *Tufts University Health & Nutrition Letter,* 7 (April 1989): 7.

(Part B)

p. 39. learned creativity with balancing spices: Archambeault, "Family Meals," 97.

p. 39. family meals taught her to prepare complex: Ibid.

p. 39. make complete last-minute meals: Ibid.

p. 39. home meals sparked her imagination: Ibid.

p. 39. inject some fun by playing: Ibid.

p. 39. helped her learn to be distinctive: Ibid.

p. 39. dinnertime conversations supporting our interest in music: Ibid.

p. 39. helped to develop a creative approach to life: Ibid., 96.

p. 39. influenced him to experiment with ingredients: Ibid.

p. 41. A meal is about civilizing children: Nancy Gibbs, "The Magic of the Family Meal," *Time*, June 4, 2006, 1, http://www.time.com/time/magazine/article/0,9171,1200760,00.html.

p. 41. If it were just about food, we would squirt it: Ibid.

p. 41. chief culture-transmitting agency: James H. S. Bossard, "Family Table Talk: An Area for Sociological Study," *American Sociological Review* 8, no. 3 (June 1943): 298.

p. 42. university seminar on family culture: Ibid., 300.

p. 42. consistent protective factor: Miriam Weinstein, *The Surprising Power of Family Meals: How Eating Together Makes Us Smarter, Stronger, Healthier and Happier* (Hanover: Steerforth, 2005), 33.

p. 43. grow our souls together: Mary Pipher, PhD, *Another Country* (New York: Riverhead Books, 1999), 273.

p. 43. Our elders have special needs and special gifts: Ibid., 306.

p. 45. Children increase their vocabulary: Susan Neuman, "Building Vocabulary to Build Literacy," *Scholastic Early Childhood Today* 21, no. 2 (October 2006): 9.

p. 46. promote language development even more than does family story reading: Carl Honoré, *Under Pressure: Rescuing our Children from the Culture of Hyper-Parenting* (New York: HarperOne, 2008), 175.

p. 46. describes this strategy to expand vocabulary: Society for the Advancement of Education, "Mealtime Conversations Help Kids Communicate," *USA Today* 124, December 1995, 3.

p. 47. fascinating chemistry lessons: "Chemistry of Cooking," *ScienceDaily.com*, January 1, 2009, http://www.sciencedaily.com/videos/2009/0112-chemistry_of_cooking.htm.

p. 48. almost twice as likely to receive As in school: The National Center on Addiction and Substance Abuse at Columbia University, "The Importance of Family Dinners," September 2003, 6.

p. 48. nearly 40 percent likelier to say they receive mostly As and Bs: "The Importance of Family Dinners II," 2005, 11.

p. 48. one and a half times likelier to report getting mostly Cs: "The Importance of Family Dinners V," 2009, 2.

p. 51. understand the link between food and spiritual connection: Waters, "The Ethics of Eating (Part 2)," 64–65.

p. 51. deeper understanding of the natural world: Michael Pollan, *Cooked: A Natural History of Transformation* (New York: Penguin Press, 2013), 2.

p. 52. informal blessing: Angela Congelose, interview with the author, December 10, 2011.

p. 52. join the metaphysical with the physical: Barbara Biziou, *The Joy of Ritual: Recipes to Celebrate Milestones, Transitions, and Everyday Events in our Lives* (New York: Golden Books Adult Publishing, 1999), 10.

p. 52. we actively participate in our own development: Ibid.

p. 52. Biziou says what makes a ritual powerful: Ibid., 15.

p. 52. it's the same thing as church: Archambeault, "Family Meals," 88.

p. 52. making the best of what you have today: Ibid.

p. 53. Small acts become ceremonial: Mary Pipher, PhD, *Another Country* (New York: Riverhead Books, 1999), 281.

Step 3: Making Room in Your Life for Shared Meals

p. 56. The very act of eating, the basis of many of our social: Roberts, *The End of Food*, xii.

p. 56. 80 percent of families believe sharing meals: Purdue University Center for Families, "Promoting Family Meals," *Center for Families* (West Lafayette, IN: Purdue University), accessed June 27, 2010, http://www.cfs. purdue.edu/cff/promotingfamilymeals.

p. 56. they are too busy with work, or there are too many different activities: "The Importance of Family Dinners V," 2009, 1.

p. 56. 65 percent of teens and 75 percent of parents: Ibid. 2.

p. 57. avoid the topic of sharing meals: Archambeault, "Family Meals," 98. Some people, including some women, may feel that women's growing presence in the workforce has caused the occurrence of sharing meals to become more infrequent. My brother Sam feels that women working outside the home has impacted family meals.

p. 57. did not vary much based on whether the mother was a working woman: Neumark-Sztainer, *"I'm, Like, SO Fat!,"* 189.

p. 58. Simplicity is the ultimate sophistication: Leonardo da Vinci, quoted on http://www.ThinkExist.com, accessed November 3, 2012, http://en.thinkexist.com/quotation/simplicity_is_the_ultimate_ sophistication/213576.html.

p. 60. Erin Callan: 'Don't Do It Like Me,'" interview by Ann Curry, *Rock Center*, NBC, March 15, 2013, http://rockcenter.nbcnews.com/_ news/2013/03/15/17301962-former-lehman-cfo-erin-callan-dont-do-it- like-me?lite.

p. 60. reasonable modifications or tweaks: Ibid.

p. 60. A recent National Study of Employers: Ellen Galinsky, James T. Bond, Kelly Sakai, Stacy S. Kim, and Nicole Giuntoli, "National Study of Employers," Families & Work Institute (2008): 3, http://www. familiesandwork.org/site/research/reports/2008nse.pdf.

p. 60. companies best achieving the ideal of making work 'work': Ibid., 43.

p. 60. what employers reported as allowed practices: Ibid., 3–4.

p. 60. 79 percent of the companies: Ibid., 6.

p. 60. culture of flexibility and supportiveness: Ibid., 26.

p. 60. although 60 percent said it was true: Ibid.

p. 60. management rewarded only 20 percent: Ibid.

p. 60. limited effort (an average of 21 percent): Ibid.

p. 61. cost and the possible loss of productivity: Ibid., 33.

p. 61. food choice coping strategies: "Work Conditions Impact Parents' Food Choices," *ScienceDaily.com*, September 15, 2009, http://www.sciencedaily.com/releases/2009/09/090909064719.htm.

p. 61. mothers were forced to compromise: Ibid.

p. 61. fathers ate while working: Ibid.

p. 62. a nation of pioneers: Jeremy Rifkin, *Time Wars* (New York: Henry Holt and Company, 1987), 64.

p. 62. shifted from the natural rhythms of life: Ibid., 117.

p. 62. single-minded value of increased efficiency: Ibid.

p. 62. a service called a work down call: Hugo Martin, "Hotel Tells Guests when It's Time to Hit the Sack," March 10, 2013, http://www.latimes.com/business/money/la-fi-mo-hotel-sleep-20130308,0,4927941.story.

p. 62. How does the decision we make today conform to the teachings: Jeremy Rifkin, *Time Wars* (New York: Henry Holt and Company, 1987), 65.

p. 63. the brain can only attend to one activity: Claudia Wallis, "The Multitasking Generation," *Time*, March 19, 2000, 4, http://www.time.com/time/magazine/article/0,9171,1174696,00.

p. 63. highly practiced skills: Ibid.

p. 63. low multitaskers have better and more cognitive control: Adam Gorlick, "Study Finds People Who Multitask Often Bad at It," August 24, 2009, http://www.physorg.com/news170349575.html.

p. 63. high multitaskers are more easily distracted: Ibid.

p. 64. natural ability to maintain concentration: Claudia Wallis, "The Multitasking Generation," *Time*, March 19, 2000, 5, http://www.time.com/time/magazine/article/0,9171,1174696,00.

p. 65. Orman also says to get your priorities: Suze Orman, *The Money Book for the Young, Fabulous and Broke* (New York: Riverhead/Penguin, 2005), 357.

p. 65. It serves as a badge of toughness: Olds and Schwartz, *The Lonely American*, 14.

p. 65. cult of conspicuous busyness: Barbara Ehrenreich, *The Worst Years of Our Lives: Irreverent Notes from a Decade of Greed* (New York: Pantheon, 1990), 23.

p. 65. society perceives someone's worth based on their degree of busyness: Ibid.

p. 65. 35 percent of the males and 42 percent of the females: "Young Adults Need to Make More Time for Healthy Meals," *ScienceDaily.com*, January 8, 2009, http://www.sciencedaily.com/releases/2009/01/090106102904.htm.

p. 66. orgy of acceleration: Honoré, *In Praise of Slowness*, 10.

p. 66. I might put on a yoga or meditation tape: Meditation and yoga have been helpful activities in achieving this peaceful state of mind. Admittedly a novice at these practices, I've still learned as much as I need to get the benefits—mindful of my energy output and thoughtfulness on quality of life balance.

p. 66. it's company for them: Archambeault, "Family Meals," 143.

p. 67. admitted eating dinner in front of the tube 42 percent: Nancy Hellmich, "Many Kids Are Eating (Too Much) in Front of TV," *USA Today*, February 14, 2001, http://www.usatoday.com/news/health/2001-02-14-kid-diet.htm.

p. 67. children who were not overweight reported eating 35 percent: Ibid.

p. 67. overweight companions ate 50 percent: Ibid.

Step 4: Aligning Values and Actions

p. 70. Nobody can go back and start a new beginning: Maria Robinson, quoted on http://www.ThinkExist.com, accessed July 13, 2010, http://en.thinkexist.com/quotation/nobody_can_go_back_and_start_a_new_beginning-but/174633.html.

p. 71. defines life balance in three dimensions: David Gruder, *The New IQ: How Integrity Intelligence Serves You, Your Relationships, and Our World* (Santa Rosa: Elite Books, 2007) 28–29.

p. 71. paradigm shift: Stephen Covey, *The 7 Habits of Highly Effective People* (New York: Free Press, 2004), 29. As Covey reports, the term "paradigm shift" was introduced by Thomas Kuhn in his book *The Structure of Scientific Revolutions*.

p. 71. sources of our attitudes about behaviors: Ibid., 30.

p. 72. voluntary simplicity: Allison Glock, "Back to Basics: Living with 'Voluntary Simplicity,'" *O, The Oprah Magazine*, December 23, 2008, http://www.oprah.com/omagazine/Meet-Followers-of-the-Simple-Living-Philosophy.

p. 72. find the satisfaction of enough: Ibid.

p. 73. benefits employers see when they offer flexibility: Kenneth Matos and Ellen Galinsky, "National Study of Employers," Families & Work Institute (2012): 2, http://www.familiesandwork.org/site/research/reports/NSE_2012.pdf.

p. 73. more likely to be in excellent physical health: Ibid.

p. 73. town hall and department meetings: Joe Light, "More Workers Start to Quit," *The Wall Street Journal* via Yahoo! Finance, May 26, 2010, http://www.finance.yahoo.com/career-work/article/109636/more-workers-start-to-quit?mod=career-worklife_balance.

p. 76. time becomes a benign element: Honoré, *In Praise of Slowness*, 279.

p. 76. Be fast when it makes sense to be fast: Ibid., 15.

p. 76. tempo giusto: Ibid.

p. 78. The challenge was a seven-day experiment: Peter Walsh, "The Family First Challenge," *Oprah.com*, January 11, 2010, http://www.oprah.com/oprahshow/Peter-Walshs-Family-First-Challenge/2.

p. 78. were so excited for this little thing: Ibid.

Step 5: Avoiding Pitfalls

p. 90. spectator sport: Michael Pollan, *Cooked: A Natural History of Transformation* (New York: Penguin Press, 2013), 3.

p. 90. Too often we let the perfect be the enemy: Mark Bittman, "Shared Meals, Shared Knowledge," *New York Times,* September 27, 2011, http://www.opinionator.blogs.nytimes.com/2011/09/27/shared-meals-shared-knowledge.

p. 93. If you drop something in the pot it's a kiss: Curtis Stone, *Relaxed Cooking with Curtis Stone: Recipes to Put You in My Favorite Mood* (New York: Clarkson Potter, 2009), 174.

p. 93. Get your hands on quality ingredients: Ibid., Introduction.

p. 93. best books I've seen for beginning cooks: Jamie Oliver, *Jamie's Food Revolution: Rediscover How to Cook Simple, Delicious, Affordable Meals* (New York: Penguin Books, 2009).

p. 93. teach it to at least two people: Ibid., 9.

Step 6: Planning and Preparing Shared Meals

p. 103. how well you believe you can perform a task: Richard I. Evans: *Albert Bandura: The Man and his Ideas—a Dialogue* (New York: Praeger Publishers, 1989), 54.

p. 106. Dora, a Reiki master: Interview with Dora Garza, interview with the author, April 28, 2013.

p. 110. restaurant industry is a $632 billion: The National Restaurant Association, accessed March 17, 2012, http://www.restaurant.org/research/facts.

p. 111. 48 percent of the food dollar: Ibid.

p. 112. find similar strategies in the book: Bob Greene, *The Get with the Program! Guide to Fast Food and Family Restaurants* (New York: Simon & Schuster, 2004), 29.

p. 112. You can develop your palate: The many ethnic restaurants that exist now offer the option of eating food that you might not be exposed to otherwise. My friend Olga and I sometimes explore new restaurants in neighborhoods we've never been to, and we are often pleasantly surprised by our culinary adventures.

p. 112. benefits of discovering new dishes: Eve Zibart, *The Ethnic Food Lover's Companion* (Birmingham, AL: Menasha Ridge Press, 2001). I read in Zibart's book that Thai food has a strong theme of *balance*, and frequently a Thai dish contains four elements—hot, sour, salty, and sweet (or *prik, preeo, khem,* and *wan*). Having this knowledge offers me a fresh perspective. I look at an order of *pad thai* differently, having this knowledge about the symbolism of balance, a concept that has meaning to me. I also learned that the cute name of *couscous* may have come from the sound of the puffs of steam escaping in the double-boiler like tool made specifically for cooking this grain.

p. 113. Barr-Anderson says television ads feature actors: "Too Much TV Linked to Future Fast-Food Intake," *ScienceDaily.com*, February 1, 2009, http://www.sciencedaily.com/releases/2009/01/090129213436.htm.

p. 113. scarce advertisements for nutritionally sound foods: Ibid.

p. 113. Preteens absorb more than 7,600 commercials: Deborah Kotz, "How to Win the Weight Battle," *US News & World Report*, August 31, 2007, http://health.usnews.com/health-news/articles/2007/08/31/how-to-win-the-weight-battle.

p. 113. Eighty percent of obese teenagers: Ibid.

p. 113. unhealthy snack foods, especially soda: Mark Hyman, *The Blood Sugar Solution: The Ultra-Healthy Program for Losing Weight, Preventing Disease and Feeling Great Now!* (New York: Hachette Book Group/Little, Brown & Company, 2012), 41.

p. 114. By FDA standards, it means: The United States Department of Agriculture (USDA) provides a handy reference on food labeling: http://www.fda.gov/AboutFDA/Transparency/Basics/ucm214868.htm.

p. 114. Some families have a no-snacking: Karen Le Billion, *French Kids Eat Everything* (New York, NY: HarperCollins, 2012). Author Karen Le Billion learned firsthand about French meal and food practices during the time her family resided in France. She wrote about her discoveries that led to sustained happy and healthy eating habits for her children and family.

p. 114. mild pangs of hunger between meals: Roberts, *The End of Food*, 96.

p. 116. purchase price of popular, processed consumer items: David L. Katz, MD, "How to Eat Healthy on a Budget," *O, The Oprah Magazine*, June 1, 2007, http://www.oprah.com/omagazine/How-to-Eat-Healthy-While-on-A-Budget.

p. 116. healthier product is only marginally more expensive: Ibid.

p. 116. current data on the dirty dozen: Environmental Working Group, http://www.ewg.org/foodnews.

p. 117. Psychologist Mihaly Csikszentmihalyi calls flow: Mihaly Csikszentmihalyi, *Flow: The Classic Work on How to Achieve Happiness* (New York: Harper Perennial, 1991), 32.

p. 117. intrinsic motivation: Alfie Kohn, *Punished by Rewards: The Trouble with Gold Stars, Incentive Plans, A's, Praise, and Other Bribes* (New York: Houghton Mifflin Company, 1993), 211–212.

p. 117. Goals achieved through intrinsic motivation: Ibid., 68.

p. 117. food people help to prepare may taste better: "Hard Work Improves the Taste of Food," Physorg.com, November 4, 2010, http://www.physorg.com/news/2010-11-hard-food.html.

p. 117. a person may eat more of it as an attempt: Ibid.

Step 7: Making Shared Meals a Sustainable Habit

p. 122. l'arte d'arrangiarsi: Elizabeth Gilbert, *Eat Pray Love* (New York: Penguin, 2006), 61.

p. 124. our moods are malleable: A. A. Labroo and A. Mukhopadhyay, "Lay Theories of Emotion Transience and the Search for Happiness: A Fresh Perspective on Affect Regulation," *Journal of Consumer Research* 36 (August 2009): 1, http://www.bm.ust.hk/mark/staff/Anirban/Anirban%20JCR-Aug%202009.pdf.

p. 124. negative moods tend to be fleeting: Ibid.

p. 126. A fifty-year study showed an association between family rituals and happier marriages: "Family Meals Lead to Healthy and Happy Children," *Bristol Evening Post*, December 10, 2002.

p. 126. Parents should choose when to eat and what to eat: Alan Lake quoted in Deborah Kotz, "How to Win the Weight Battle," *US News and World Report*, August 31, 2007, http:// health.usnews.com/health-news/articles/2007/08/31/how-to-win-the-weight-battle?page=4.

p. 130. the practices you keep when feeding your child: Ellyn Satter, *Child of Mine: Feeding with Love and Good Sense* (Palo Alto, CA: Bull Publishing Company, 2000), 202.

p. 130. For your child's eating to turn out well: Ibid., 337.

p. 131. authoritative style of parenting is best: "Authoritative Parenting Style Influences Family Eating Behavior and Better Nutrition in Adolescents," *ScienceDaily.com*, July 1, 2010, http://www.sciencedaily.com/releases/2010/07/100701081851.htm.

p. 131. Parents who were empathic and respectful: Ibid.

Bibliography

Archambeault, Carol. "Family Meals: A Multigenerational Perspective on the Developmental Impact of the Family Meal Ritual." master's thesis, Pacific Oaks College, December 2007.

Bittman, Mark. *Food Matters: A Guide to Conscious Eating with More Than 75 Recipes.* New York: Simon & Schuster, 2009.

Biziou, Barbara. *The Joy of Ritual: Recipes to Celebrate Milestones, Transitions, and Everyday Events in our Lives.* New York: Golden Books Adult Publishing, 1999.

Bolton, Robert. *People Skills: How to Assert Yourself, Listen to Others, and Resolve Conflicts.* New York: Simon & Schuster, 1979.

Bossard, James H. S. "Family Table Talk: An Area for Sociological Study." *American Sociological Review* 8, no. 3 (June 1943): 295-301.

Brown, Brené. "The Power of Vulnerability," TEDxHouston video, 20:21. June 2010. http://www.ted.com/talks/brene_brown_on_vulnerability.html.

Buettner, Dan. *The Blue Zone: Lessons for Living Longer from the People Who've Lived the Longest.* Washington DC: National Geographic, 2008.

Callan, Erin. "Former Lehman CFO Erin Callan: Don't Do It Like Me," By Ann Curry, *Rock Center*, NBC (March 15, 2013).

Centers for Disease Control and Prevention. "Adult Obesity: Obesity Rises Among Adults," August 2010.

—. "Childhood Overweight and Obesity," *National Health and Nutrition Examination Survey*, 2007-2008.

—. "Eating Behaviors of Young People," 2013.

Cote, James. *Arrested Adulthood: The Changing Nature of Maturity and Identity.* New York: New York University, 2000.

Covey, Stephen. *The 7 Habits of Highly Effective People.* New York: Free Press, 2004.

Csikszentmihalyi, Mihaly. *Flow: the Classic Work on How to Achieve Happiness.* New York: Harper Perennial, 1991.

Ehrenreich, Barbara. *The Worst Years of Our Lives: Irreverent Notes from a Decade of Greed.* New York: Pantheon, 1990.

Eisenberg, Marla, Rachel Olson, Dianne Neumark-Sztainer, Mary Story, and Linda Bearinger. "Correlations between Family Meals and Psychosocial Well-Being among Adolescents," *Archives of Pediatrics and Adolescent Medicine* 158, no. 8 (August 2004): 792-796.

Evans, Richard I. *Albert Bandura: The Man and his Ideas—a Dialogue.* New York: Praeger Publishers, a div. of Greenwood Press, 1989.

Federal Trade Commission. "Marketing Food to Children and Adolescents: A Review of Industry Expenditures, Activities, and Self-Regulation: A Report to Congress," July 2008: 1-120.

Fisher, Mary Frances Kennedy. *The Art of Eating.* New York: Vintage Books, 1976.

The Friedman School of Science and Policy. "Families That Eat Together." *Tufts University Health & Nutrition Letter,* 15 (October 1997).

Galinsky, Ellen, James T. Bond, Kelly Sakai, Stacy S. Kim, and Nicole Giuntoli. "National Study of Employers." Families & Work Institute, 2008: 1-44.

Gibbs, Nancy. "The Magic of the Family Meal." *Time,* June 4, 2006.

Gilbert, Elizabeth. *Eat Pray Love.* New York: Penguin, 2006.

Gilligan, Carol. *In a Different Voice.* Cambridge, MA: Harvard University Press, 1993.

Goleman, Daniel. "What Is Social Intelligence?" *Greater Good,* Fall/ Winter 2006-2007: http://www.greatergood.berkeley.edu/article/ item/what_is_social_intelligence.

Gorlick, Adam. "Study Finds People Who Multitask Often Bad at It." *PhysOrg.com,* August 24, 2009.

Glock, Allison. "Back to Basics: Living with "'Voluntary Simplicity.'" *O, The Oprah Magazine,* December 23, 2008.

Greene, Bob. *The Get with the Program! Guide to Fast Food and Family Restaurants.* New York: Simon & Schuster, 2004.

Gruder, David. *The New IQ: How Integrity Intelligence Serves You, Your Relationships, and Our World.* Santa Rosa: Elite Books, 2007.

Gurian, Michael. A *Fine Young Man.* New York: Tarcher/Putnam, 1998.

"Hard Work Improves the Taste of Food," November 4, 2010, *PhysOrg.com,* November 9, 2010.

Harper, Charles L., and Bryan F. Le Beau. *Food, Society, and Environment.* Upper Saddle River, NJ: Prentice Hall, 2003.

Hellmich, Nancy. "Many Kids Are Eating (Too Much) in Front of TV." *USA Today*, February 14, 2001.

Honoré, Carl. *In Praise of Slowness: How a Worldwide Movement Is Challenging the Cult of Speed.* New York: HarperCollins, 2004.

—. *Under Pressure: Rescuing our Children from the Culture of Hyper-Parenting.* New York: HarperOne, 2008.

Hudson, Frederic M. *The Adult Years: Mastering the Art of Self-Renewal.* San Francisco: Jossey-Bass, 1999.

Hyman, Mark. *The Blood Sugar Solution: The Ultra-Healthy Program for Losing Weight, Preventing Disease and Feeling Great Now!* New York: Hachette Book Group/Little, Brown & Company, 2012.

"In Case You Haven't Heard." *Mental Health Weekly* 12, no. 7 (February 18, 2002).

Ishige, Naomichi. "Table Manners Makyth Man: The Emergence of Homo sapiens as Convivial Animal." *Unesco Courier*, May 1987.

Jackson, Elizabeth G. "Family Meals More Important than Nutritional Perfection." *Environmental Nutrition* 13, no. 9 (1990).

Katz, David L. "How to Eat Healthy on a Budget." *O, The Oprah Magazine*, June 1, 2007.

Kingsolver, Barbara. *Animal, Vegetable, Miracle.* New York: HarperCollins, 2007.

Klinenberg, Eric. "Living Alone Is the New Norm." *Time*, March 12, 2012.

Kluger, Jeffrey, Christine Gorman, and Alice Park. "America's Obesity Crisis: Eating Behavior: Why We Eat." *Time*, June 7, 2004.

Kohn, Alfie. *Punished by Rewards: The Trouble with Gold Stars, Incentive Plans, A's, Praise, and Other Bribes*. New York: Houghton Mifflin Company, 1993.

Kotz, Deborah. "How to Win the Weight Battle." *US News & World Report*, August 31, 2007. http://health.usnews.com/health-news/articles/2007/08/31/how-to-win-the-weight-battle.

Kula, Irwin Kula. "Faith and Doubt at Ground Zero." By Helen Whitney. *Frontline*, Act 2, PBS (September 3, 2002).

Labroo, A. A., and A. Mukhopadhyay. "Lay Theories of Emotion Transience and the Search for Happiness: A Fresh Perspective on Affect Regulation." *Journal of Consumer Research* 36 (August 2009): 1-13.

Larson, Nicole, Dianne Neumark-Stzainer, Peter J. Hannan, and Mary Story. "Family Meals during Adolescence Are Associated with Higher Diet Quality and Healthful Meal Patterns during Young Adulthood." *Journal of the American Dietetic Association* 107, no. 9 (September 2007): 1502-1510.

Le Billion, Karen. *French Kids Eat Everything*. New York: HarperCollins, 2012.

Matos, Kenneth and Ellen Galinsky. "National Study of Employers," Families & Work Institute, 2012: 1-54.

The National Center on Addiction and Substance Abuse at Columbia University. "The Importance of Family Dinners," September 2003.

—. "The Importance of Family Dinners II, September 2005.

—. "The Importance of Family Dinners V," September 2009.

National Eating Disorders Association (NEDA). "Facts and Statistics," nationaleatingdisorders.org.

Neuman, Susan. "Building Vocabulary to Build Literacy." *Scholastic Early Childhood Today* 21, no. 2 (October 2006).

Neumark-Sztainer, Dianne. *"I'm, Like, SO Fat!" Helping Your Teen Make Healthy Choices about Eating and Exercise in a Weight-Obsessed World.* New York: The Guilford Press, 2005.

Nudo, Lori. "Make a Dinner Date Tonight! Sit-down Meals Feed Healthy Habits. *Prevention* 54, no. 48 (July 2002).

Olds, Jacqueline, and Richard S. Schwartz. *The Lonely American: Drifting Apart in the Twenty-first Century.* Boston: Beacon Press, 2009.

Oliver, Jamie. *Jamie's Food Revolution: Rediscover How to Cook Simple, Delicious Affordable Meals.* New York: Penguin Books, 2009.

—. "Teach Every Child about Food." Ted2010 video, 21:53. February 2010. http://www.ted.com/talks/jamie_oliver.html.

Orman, Suze. *The Money Book for the Young, Fabulous and Broke.* New York: Riverhead/Penguin, 2005.

Pipher, Mary. *Another Country.* New York: Riverhead Books, 1999.

Pollan, Michael. *Cooked: A Natural History of Transformation.* New York: Penguin Press, 2013.

Purdue University Center for Families. "Promoting Family Meals." *Center for Families.* West Lafayette, IN: Purdue University, 2012.

Putnam, Robert. *Bowling Alone: The Collapse and Revival of American Community.* New York: Simon & Schuster, 2000.

Rifkin, Jeremy. *Time Wars*. New York: Henry Holt and Company, 1987.

Roberts, Paul. *The End of Food*. New York: Houghton Mifflin, 2008.

Roberts, Paul. "The New Food Anxiety." *Psychology Today*. March 1, 1998: 30-39.

Satir, Virginia. *The New Peoplemaking*. Mountain View, CA: Science and Behavior Books, 1988.

Satter, Ellyn. *Child of Mine: Feeding with Love and Good Sense*. Palo Alto, CA: Bull Publishing Company, 2000.

ScienceDaily.com; "Authoritative Parenting Style Influences Family Eating Behavior and Better Nutrition in Adolescents." July 1, 2010.

—. "Can Money Buy Happiness? Gallup Poll Asks, and the World Answers." July 2, 2010.

—. "Chemistry of Cooking." July 7, 2010.

—. "Regular Family Meals Result in Better Eating Habits for Adolescents." March 10, 2009.

—. "Share and Share Alike." August 25, 2009.

—. "Too Much TV Linked to Future Fast-Food Intake." February 1, 2009.

—. "Work Conditions Impact Parents' Food Choices," September 15, 2009.

—. "Young Adults Need to Make More Time for Healthy Meals." January 8, 2009.

Shall We Dance, DVD. Directed by Peter Chelsom. Santa Monica, CA: Miramax Films, 2004.

Society for the Advancement of Education. "Mealtime Conversations Help Kids Communicate." *USA Today,* 124, December 1995.

Spiegel, Lynn. *Make Room for TV: Television and the Family Ideal in Postwar America.* Chicago: University of Chicago Press, 1992.

Stone, Curtis. *Relaxed Cooking with Curtis Stone: Recipes to Put You in My Favorite Mood.* New York: Clarkson Potter, 2009.

Story, Mary, and Jamie Stang. "Understanding Adolescent Eating Behaviors." *Guidelines for Adolescent Nutrition Services.* Minneapolis: Center for Leadership, Education, and Training in Maternal and Child Nutrition, Division of Epidemiology and Community Health, School of Public Health, University of Minnesota, 2005: 9-19.

Tufts University. "For Senior Ctizens Who Live Alone." *Tufts University Health & Nutrition Letter,* 7 (April 1989).

Wallis, Claudia. "The Multitasking Generation." *Time*, March 19, 2006.

Walsh, Peter. "The Family First Challenge." Oprah.com, January 11, 2010.

Waters, Alice. "The Ethics of Eating (Part 2)." *Whole Earth 90* (Summer 1997).

Weinstein, Miriam. *The Surprising Power of Family Meals: How Eating Together Makes Us Smarter, Stronger, Healthier and Happier.* Hanover: Steerforth, 2005.

Zibart, Eve. *The Ethnic Food Lover's Companion.* Birmingham, AL: Menasha Ridge Press, 2001.

About the Author

In *The Shared-Meal Revolution: How to Reclaim Balance and Connection in a Fragmented World through Sharing Meals with Family and Friends*, Carol Archambeault explains how sharing meals is fundamental to achieving life balance and creating meaningful interpersonal connection with those we love.

Carol was born in Connecticut as the youngest sibling in a family of four sisters and six brothers (including her twin brother). She was raised by loving parents in a household where food and family intertwined. When she became a mother, she continued the shared-meal ritual as a way to foster development of her own daughter and son.

When Carol planned the research for her graduate thesis, she landed on her own family as the perfect source for a multigenerational study. This effort revealed a deeper understanding of how the shared-meal ritual impacts family members from early childhood through late adulthood.

The Shared-Meal Revolution is the result of both research and inspiration. After receiving her MA in human development in 2007 from Pacific Oaks College (California), Carol became motivated to continue her work on shared meals to promote a universal understanding of how a shared-meal ritual can enhance the lives of individuals, families, communities . . . and American society.

Currently residing in Los Angeles, California, Carol shares ideas and stories about creating rich meal and lifestyle experiences in her blog *Shared Meals Matter,* on her website www.shared-meals.com, as well as through articles in online and print media.

Carol enjoys dual citizenship in Italy and is working on her next book, which explores shared-meal practices in other countries. The working title is *Sharing Meals—Global to Local.*

CPSIA information can be obtained at www.ICGtesting.com
Printed in the USA
BVOW08s1923271113

337558BV00001B/4/P